Budgeting for Profit

How to Exploit the Potential of Your Business

An Alexander Hamilton Institute Book
Chilton's Better Business Series

Budgeting for Profit

How to Exploit the Potential of Your Business

John C. Camillus

University of Pittsburgh

CHILTON BOOK COMPANY
RADNOR, PENNSYLVANIA

Copyright © 1982, 1984 by Alexander Hamilton Institute, Inc.
Modern Business Reports, 1633 Broadway, New York, NY 10019
All Rights Reserved
Published in Radnor, Pennsylvania 19089, by Chilton Book Company
Designed by Jean Callan King/Metier Industrial, Inc.
Manufactured in the United States of America

Library of Congress Cataloging in Publication Data
Camillus, John C.
    Budgeting for profit.
    (Chilton's better business series)
    Includes index.
    1. Budget in business.   2. Corporate planning.
I. Title.   II. Series.
HG4028.B8C35   1984   658.1'54   84-1819
ISBN 0-8019-7523-9 (pbk.)

Chilton's Better Business Series

1 2 3 4 5 6 7 8 9 0   3 1 0 9 8 7 6 5 4

Contents

List of Figures

List of Tables

Introduction

Planning and control are key functions for all executives. And a profitable performance is a key requirement for all companies. "Budgeting For Profit: How to Exploit the Potential of Your Business" provides you with a powerful and proven budgeting system to accomplish these two objectives.

That profit budgeting system is designed with one fundamental purpose—to enable your firm to identify and exploit its profit potential more effectively than it has in the past.

Based on the practical experiences of companies in a number of different industries, the system includes the best aspects from a variety of effective budgeting programs in use today.

By incorporating the practices recommended in this book, you'll be able to:

- integrate individual department budgets into a complete company-wide system;

- assess the quality of your current reporting system and promote increased communication throughout the business;

- encourage and promote improved managerial performance;
- pinpoint areas of overlapping authority in order to create a more rational organization structure;
- install a successful system without demanding extensive, added technical expertise from current executives or the utilization of outside consultants;
- develop the analytical capabilities of your managers and broaden their perspectives;
- analyze the financial status of your own firm and that of its major competitors.

More than 35 charts, diagrams and tables graphically complement the text with easy-to-follow numbers and sample explanations. These illustrations give the entire process a "true-to-life" appearance, as well as provide you with applicable documents to use when implementing your own program.

Among the forms you'll find are responsibility center classifications, an environmental analysis matrix, actual performance reports for a manufacturing manager, recommended budget formats, and specific action plans.

"Budgeting For Profit" even takes you through the step-by-step process of developing a system for a hypothetical manufacturing firm— General Meters Corporation. In that way you can see how the contents of the book can be matched with the structure of your own company.

Each Section leads into the next in a tightly-woven series of explanations that culminate with "Action Requirements." These will show you how to use the information included in each successive Section.

The final Section helps you set up your own method for monitoring and reviewing what you have accomplished.

This manual will cover everything you need to know to install your own profit-oriented budgeting system—including the who, when, where and why—but most importantly, the HOW.

John C. Camillus, B. Tech., PGDBM, D.B.A., Associate Dean of the Graduate School of Business at the University of Pittsburgh, developed this special report in conjunction with the editors of the Alexander Hamilton Institute.

Professor Camillus received his Doctoral Degree from the Graduate School of Business Administration at Harvard University.

An acknowledged expert in the field, Professor Camillus has written or collaborated on over 20 articles and books on management planning and control. He has been a consultant to numerous organizations and has conducted business research projects in both developed and developing countries.

Budgeting
for Profit

How to Exploit the Potential of Your Business

I

Background to Budgeting for Profit

Budgets have been an important and widely-used management tool for the past 40 years. In the 1950's, highly financially-oriented budgets intended primarily for cost control were prepared by a firm's accountants. These proved inadequate since they failed to recognize human factors and were unable to cope with the increasingly dynamic business environment.

Long-range planning systems were developed in the 1960's which typically offered financial projections over a five-year period. They failed to assist managers in identifying and responding to opportunities and problems in a timely and effective manner.

In the 1970's, strategic planning systems emerged. Techniques developed for analyzing the company and its environment in more powerful ways. The problem with these seemingly impressive systems was the difficulty many companies had translating such plans into reality.

The latest trend emphasizes annual "strategic" business plans that strike a compromise between short-term financial budgets and long-range strategic plans. The resulting system designs are similar to the profit budgeting system explained in this book.

ADDRESSING THE BUDGETING PROCESS

The approach is basically simple. First, a method is developed that provides the outline for the budgeting system. Each subunit of the firm—production, marketing, finance, personnel and other departments—is classified according to a particular scheme.

After the classification comes the second step which enables you to uncover the best way to describe and measure the performance of each subunit or department, and the company as a whole. Many firms already have good information and reporting systems to measure such performance.

Besides providing a framework for speedily identifying possible weaknesses in your existing reporting systems, this system will also provide you with lists of possible indicators or measures to add to existing reports to create comprehensive and up-to-date designs.

The third step, specifying performance levels, involves three stages. You'll learn:

1. Various methods for setting performance standards for activities carried out within the departments in your company. Plus how to select the most suitable method for each particular situation.

2. How to set performance expectations for each type of department in your firm, such as production, marketing, and others.

3. A novel and effective way to set profit targets for the company as a whole. As well as what you need to analyze, who should carry out the various analyses, what the budget document should contain, and how to tailor your profit target to best suit your managers and your company.

The next step after specifing performance levels is monitoring and reviewing actual performance with respect to the standards, expectations and profit targets already set. You'll find practical and proven guidelines to insure efficient managerial control and effective remedial action.

Finally comes the implementation of the new system of budgeting for profit. Whether you already have reporting and budget systems, or are considering an initial introduction of such formal systems, the explanation of this exercise will be helpful.

II

Analyzing the Organization Structure

To develop the best budgeting system for planning and controlling your firm's profits, you must be able to describe the various operations in a suitable manner.

THE INPUT-PROCESS-OUTPUT MODEL

Visualize your firm as a mechanism or process that converts inputs such as money, human effort and raw materials, into desired outputs, such as profits. The executive exercises control over the inputs and process and is responsible for generating the desired output, as pictured in Table 1.

Most modern firms do not allow a single manager to make all the decisions needed to convert inputs efficiently and effectively into profits. So the firm is divided into simpler, more homogenous subunits, functions or departments.

Each of these departments can be viewed as a process of converting inputs into desired outputs. Thus, the manufacturing department

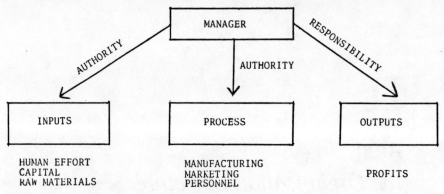

Table 1. The input-process-output model

converts raw materials and power into finished goods; the marketing department converts these finished goods into dollars of revenue; the personnel department converts job applicants into machinists and salespeople, and so forth.

But each department is very different from the others. These differences are important for planning and control. The planned workload of some departments, such as manufacturing, is based on desired output. The workload in other departments, such as legal or maintenance, is based on inputs such as lawsuits or job requisitions.

The outputs of certain departments are tangible and readily measurable. The outputs of other departments are hard to describe or objectively measure. It is necessary, therefore, to classify subunits into categories that permit similar approaches to planning and control. One such generalized classification scheme is the "Process-Output Matrix."

THE PROCESS-OUTPUT MATRIX

When designing appropriate planning and control mechanisms, the most important attribute of each department is whether its outputs are quantifiable and measurable. The manufacturing department and the marketing department are examples where you can readily measure outputs (units of production and dollars of revenue).

On the other hand, the accounting and finance department and the personnel and industrial relations department, generate outputs

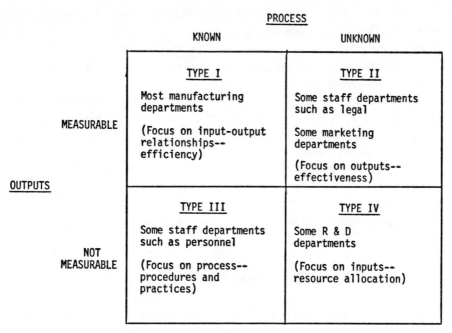

Figure 1. Four types of departments in the process-out matrix

(managerial information and industrial harmony) that are often intangible and difficult to quantify and measure.

A second major distinguishing attribute among various types of departments is whether the processes they employ are well-defined and understood. For instance, assembly operations in manufacturing are generally carefully defined and easily understood. But creating advertising copy or designing a new product are relatively undefined and not clearly understood processes in most situations.

Considering these attributes, the process-output matrix in Figure 1 identifies four types of departments.

Type I departments are those in which the process is known and the outputs are measurable. They are the easiest to manage and evaluate, and can be tightly controlled. Efficiency (the relationship between inputs and outputs) is the primary focus of budgeting systems for these departments.

Type II departments, where the process is unknown but outputs can be measured, require control mechanisms that focus on the extent to which desired outputs are achieved. A company as a whole would possess the characteristics of a Type II unit. The numerous and complex processes and decisions involved in managing the firm may not be totally understood or clearly defined, but the end result or outputs appear quite clearly on financial statements.

Type III departments are difficult to manage. While you can focus on whether accepted practices and procedures are carried out carefully and in a timely manner, it is often impossible to ascertain whether the desired results are being obtained.

Type IV departments are typified by Research and Development (R&D) departments oriented toward basic rather than applied research. Since both process and outputs are unclear, you must try to manage the quantity and quality of inputs or resources provided to these departments.

GENERAL METERS CORPORATION

A hypothetical firm, General Meters Corporation (GMC), demonstrates the application of the above classification scheme. GMC manufactures two product lines, water meters and gas meters. All manufacturing activities are carried out in one plant located in an eastern coastal city. The plant is run by a manufacturing manager and has four major departments—foundry, machining, assembly, and maintenance.

Sales are the responsibility of the marketing manager who has two product managers report to him. The two product managers are responsible for residential and industrial sales respectively. The president/general manager directly supervises the manufacturing manager and marketing manager. In addition, the chief accountant and the personnel manager also report to the president/general manager. Figure 2 is an organization chart for GMC.

MANUFACTURING RESPONSIBILITY CENTERS

The term "responsibility center" refers to those subunits which have a manager-supervisor with well-defined authority and responsibility. Three of the four responsiblity centers in GMC's manufacturing area—foundry, machine shop and assembly shop—are clearly Type I units. Their inputs

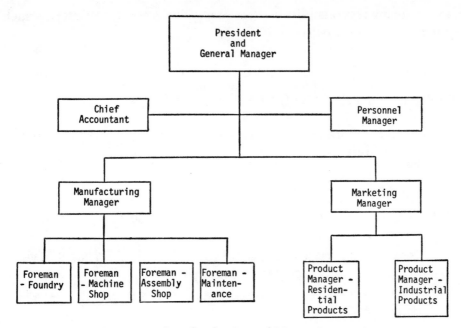

Figure 2. An organization chart for the General Meters Corporation

(raw materials, components, supplies, labor, utilities) and outputs (components, finished goods) are well-defined and readily measurable.

Moreover, the processes which convert the inputs into outputs are well-defined and understood. As a consequence, you should be able to determine objectively the appropriate amount of inputs needed to generate a required amount of outputs. You can thus specify the efficiency (output ÷ input) with which these three departments should operate.

Another important characteristic of these three responsibility centers is that you can measure the inputs they require (raw materials, components, supplies, labor, utilities, etc.) in monetary terms. So the monetary value of all the inputs required by these responsiblity centers can be determined.

It is difficult to assign a monetary value to their outputs. Cost figures are generally misleading because they usually include arbitrary allocations of costs and represent a certain method of attaching costs to products rather than an objective, defensible, economic valuation of those products. You can, however, measure the outputs of these three manufacturing responsiblity centers in physical, quantitative terms such as kilograms or number of units.

DETERMINING EXPENSE CENTERS

The important characteristics of these three manufacturing responsibility centers are:

1. Their inputs are objectively and easily measurable in monetary terms.
2. Their outputs are objectively and easily measurable in quantitative, physical (but not monetary) terms.
3. The processes by which they convert inputs into outputs are well-defined and understood.
4. The optimal relationship between inputs consumed and outputs generated can be specified.
5. They basically belong to the Type I category of the process-output matrix.

Responsibility centers which display these characteristics are also called "engineered expense centers." The budgeting systems for all engineered expense centers are remarkably similar, regardless of whether they belong to a manufacturing, marketing or finance function.

The maintenance shop is different from the other three responsibility centers reporting to the manufacturing manager. The functions and processes of the maintenance shop change depending on the nature of break-downs, necessary repairs, and specified preventive maintenance activities. The relationship between inputs and outputs cannot be easily labeled since you don't know in advance exactly what the demands on the maintenance shop will be.

All four responsibility centers in the manufacturing area are expense centers because inputs are measured in dollar terms and their outputs are measured in physical terms. But since the optimal relationship between inputs and outputs cannot be readily and objectively determined in the case of the maintenance shop, it is not an engineered expense center. It is called a discretionary expense center. Another example of a discretionary expense center would be the personnel department.

MARKETING RESPONSIBILITY CENTERS

The two product managers deal with different types of products and customers, and have different responsibilities. The product manager-residential products sells a standard line of water and gas meters for household use to plumbing and building supply distributors throughout the country, but primarily on the east coast.

Six salesmen report to this product manager. Wholesale list prices are set by the marketing manager and the price list is updated annually. The salesmen visit the distributors and obtain orders which are transmitted back to the product manager who initiates the packing and shipping activity. He also maintains personal contact through visits to the major distributors.

The product manager-industrial products operates in a very different fashion. Sales are made directly to end-users. Orders are often obtained through a competitive bidding process. Meters often have to be custom-tailored to the client's specifications. No formal pricelist is printed because of the number and type of variations in design specifications.

Brochures describing the types of meters that GMC can make are printed and distributed to former customers. Advertisements in industry and trade journals induce inquiries from prospective customers.

The product manager-industrial products determines the price quotations for prospective customers. Every few months, the marketing manager reviews those prices.

The product manager-industrial products has three senior, technical salespeople reporting to him, stationed in various sectors of the country. Together they keep in touch with the purchasing and technical personnel of prospective clients and explain the superior technical characteristics of GMC meters.

TWO DIFFERENT BUDGETING APPROACHES

These two marketing responsibility centers are clearly quite different, requiring different approaches to budgeting.

The product manager-residential products has no authority over the pricing decision. His responsibility is to generate the maximum amount of unit sales within the constraints of the output of the manufacturing function. His outputs are dollars of sales revenue. His inputs are the efforts that he and his salesmen invest in their dealings with the distributors, and the meters provided to him for sale.

The salary paid to his salesmen and himself can be viewed as a measure of their efforts but this has obvious shortcomings. The goods provided to him for sale can be valued at cost, which is arbitrary, or at list price, which is inappropriate since he has no margin for profit.

This responsibility center is very similar to the expense centers in manufacturing. Here the inputs are not readily measurable in monetary terms and the outputs are best expressed in dollars of revenue. This kind of responsibility center is called a "revenue center."

Note that revenue centers are Type II subunits in that their outputs are measurable, but the process by which the outputs are generated is not well-defined. The planning and control system for such revenue centers would therefore focus on the level of output generated, with only secondary attention to the relationship between inputs and outputs.

The product manager-industrial products has one important decision which makes his responsibility center very different from the residential products center. He controls the pricing decision. That means that he can influence the dollars or revenue generated by manipulating two factors—price and volume. The product manager-residential products can affect revenue by manipulating only one factor—volume—because the pricing decision is made by the marketing manager.

ATTRIBUTES OF A CONTRIBUTION CENTER

The control of price and volume makes the industrial products center more complex than a revenue center. Should advertising expenditures be increased if additional revenue can be generated by increased prices that are made possible because of a better image? If 10,000 units of a meter can be sold at $15 a meter and 15,000 units can be sold at $10 a meter, what is the correct decision?

The product manager-industrial products must balance inputs and outputs to arrive at the most profitable combination of selling price, marketing costs and units sold. To evaluate this responsiblity center primarily on revenue generated would be undesirable. You must determine the contribution to the firm's profits made by this responsibility center.

To summarize, the important characteristics of a revenue center are:

1. The inputs are objectively and easily measurable in quantitative, physical (but not monetary) terms.
2. The outputs are objectively and easily measurable in monetary terms.
3. The process by which inputs are converted into outputs is not very well-defined and individual salespeople can employ subtly or radically different methods.
4. The focus of planning and control is on the outputs (revenue) generated, in the context of a given quantity of goods being available for sale.
5. The center basically belongs to the Type II category of the process output matrix.

The important characteristics of a contribution center are:

1. It is basically a revenue center where the inputs are converted to a monetary value by the use of an appropriately determined transfer price for valuing the goods provided by manufacturing to the center.
2. The focus of planning and control is on the difference between the revenue generated and the costs incurred, i.e., the contribution to the firm's profits made by the center.
3. It is again, basically, a Type II subunit as defined in the process-output matrix.

To do this, you place an appropriate value on the meters supplied to this department. This type of responsibility center is called a *"contribution center."* Both the inputs (marketing expenses, goods provided for sale) and outputs (revenue generated) are measurable in monetary terms. In such a center, you calculate the contribution to corporate profits as the difference between the revenue generated and the cost incurred—including the cost of the meters supplied by the manufacturing department.

STAFF AND SERVICE RESPONSIBILITY CENTERS

The maintenance shop, personnel department and accounting department are Type III subunits. Their outputs are difficult to measure, but the activities or processes they are expected to carry out are fairly well-defined. For all of them, however, their inputs are readily measurable in monetary terms. They are therefore also expense centers.

An important difference between these expense centers and the three other expense centers (foundry, machine shop and assembly shop) is that the relationship between inputs and outputs in the case of staff and service units is a matter of judgment. You cannot determine the amount of money that the personnel manager should spend on salaries and wages, supplies, and so forth by means of a formula.

Managerial discretion must be exercised, for instance, regarding the caliber and quality of people hired to perform the activities in these staff and service units. Consequently, these expense centers, where the amount of inputs consumed in order to generate the desired, often intangible outputs is a matter of judgment, are called "discretionary expense centers."

THE COMPANY AS A RESPONSIBILITY CENTER

The company as a whole has characteristics different from the responsibility centers already discussed. In essence, the firm is the sum of all the responsibility centers within it. The inputs employed by the firm as a whole are best measured in monetary terms. Its outputs are represented by the profit that it generates. The firm as a whole is appropriately labeled a "profit center." It is essentially a Type II unit in that the process

The characteristics of these discretionary expense centers are:

1. Their inputs are objectively and easily measurable in monetary terms.
2. Their outputs are difficult to measure, often intangible and cannot be measured in monetary terms.
3. The processes by which inputs are converted into outputs are usually not well-defined.
4. The optimal relationship between inputs and outputs cannot be specified objectively.
5. They usually belong to the Type III category of the process-output matrix.

by which profits are generated is complex and cannot readily be identified, while the outputs are quantifiable and measurable.

The key to designing a budgeting system for a profit center lies in creating a process that:

1. identifies the range of alternatives available to the firm and selects the alternative that represents the optimal matching of the firm's resources and environmental opportunities;
2. precisely defines what is expected of managers of responsibility centers to ensure that each supports the other in the implementation of the chosen alternative;
3. recognizes and responds to shortcomings within the firm or changes in its environment so that necessary mid-course corrections can be made; and
4. accomplishes all this while recognizing that human beings with a variety of motivations and capabilities are involved.

ACTION REQUIREMENTS

You should now be able to identify and classify the responsibility centers in your organization. Remember, a responsibility center *must* have a

1) Engineered Expense Centers (Type I)

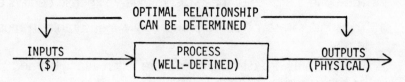

2) Discretionary Expense Centers (Mostly Type III)

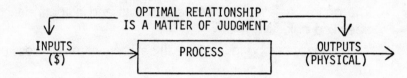

3) Revenue Centers (Type II)

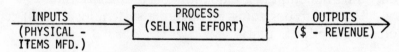

4) Contribution Centers (Type II)

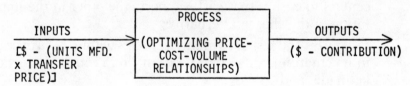

5) Profit Center (Essentially Type II)

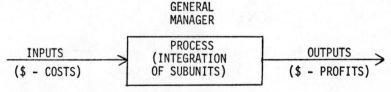

Figure 3. A graphic illustration of five types of centers

CLASSIFICATION OF GMC RESPONSIBILITY CENTERS

RESPONSIBILITY CENTER	MANAGER	CLASSIFICATION	TYPE
Foundry	Foreman	Engineered expense center	I
Machine shop	Foreman	Engineered expense center	I
Assembly shop	Foreman	Engineered expense center	I
Maintenance	Foreman	Discretionary expense center	III
Manufacturing	Manufacturing manager	Primarily an engineered expense center with discretionary elements	I/II
Residential sales	Product manager	Revenue center	II
Industrial sales	Product manager	Contribution center	II
Marketing	Marketing manager	Contribution center	II
Accounting	Chief accountant	Discretionary expense center	III
Personnel	Personnel manager	Discretionary expense center	III
GMC	General manager	Profit center	II

Figure 4. Classification of GMC responsibility centers

manager in charge and should have a significant material influence on your profit picture. Your accounting reports and other formal information will help you isolate and describe the performance of all responsibility centers.

After you identify your responsibility centers, you can then classify them according to Figure 3. Your first attempt to classify responsibility centers will necessarily be tentative. As you read the rest of the book, it will become apparent whether certain responsibility centers need to be created, or whether what is presently a revenue center should be converted into a contribution center, and so forth.

The classification, though it requires judgment, is important. You will eventually select planning and control techniques for each center based on whether it is an engineered expense center, discretionary expense center, revenue center or contribution center.

Figure 4 identifies and classifies the responsiblity centers at GMC. You can create a similar form for your own company.

III

Evaluating Your Information System

A budgeting system relies on a company's information-reporting system the same way the body relies on the skeleton for support. You cannot construct a truly effective budgeting system unless your reporting systems are also well-designed. If a good information system already exists in your organization, you can use the information in this section to fine-tune it and provide a better foundation for the budgeting system. If your firm does not already possess such a system, the information will enable you to speedily install a simple but effective series of reports.

> Note: It is important to recognize that an information system cannot and should not be designed to meet a firm's *total* information needs. When designing information systems for corporations in the public sector (government-owned) in India, we frequently were asked whether the management information system (MIS) would enable the corporation to answer questions asked by members of Parliament. To try to anticipate the range of possible questions emerging from the variety of motivations of members of Parliament would have

meant systems of such inordinate complexity and cost that they would eventually be unworkable.

CATEGORIZING INFORMATION

In identifying a feasible and appropriate focus for the MIS, keep in mind three characteristics of information required to manage a successful company.

First, the information can be quantitative and objective or qualitative and subjective. Second, it can be required routinely and regularly or non-routinely and unpredictably. Third, the information can be derived from internal or external sources.

The first characteristic (quantitative/qualitative) is important because quantitative information is easier to verify, aggregate and handle with electronic data-processing equipment. Whether the information is routine or non-routine is important because including non-routine information of unpredictable value in the system is difficult and expensive. Finally, you can more easily fashion internal information to meet your company's requirements in terms of content, frequency and availability.

Table 2 classifies these three important characteristics of information requirements into eight categories. The single most important category is quantitative, routine internal information (shaded box).

HANDLING INFORMATION

Qualitative information is best handled through oral communications and informal letters and memos at specified intervals from managers.

At General Meters Corporation (GMC), qualitative information is communicated from each subordinate to his superior when performance review meetings are held. In addition, the senior salespeople reporting to the product manager-industrial products are required to write monthly or quarterly letters to the product manager, in addition to the routine weekly and monthly quantitative reports.

Those letters focus on prospective new customers, expected requests for quotations in the next month or quarter, competitors' activities, customers' reactions to advertisements, product design and quality,

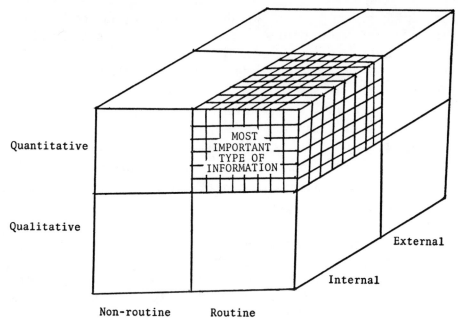

Table 2. Key characteristics of management information

and any other developments that may be of value in planning the manufacture and marketing of industrial meters.

You should generally exclude non-routine information from the formal data base of the MIS. Most non-routine information is required during annual strategic planning or profit planning exercises, or when unexpected problems or opportunities arise.

To include all conceivable information requirements in the formal MIS is highly undesirable and violates basic design principles.

IDENTIFYING INFORMATION REQUIREMENTS

In order to identify the quantitative, routine, internal information needed to plan and control the firm's operations, the input-process-output model of the firm and its responsibility centers is valuable.

After identifying the responsibility centers in your company, you should then select one of the lowest level centers. In the case of GMC, we can select the foundry or machine shop or either of the product managers. In selecting one responsibility center in your firm, it may be best to choose a center with whose operations you are most familiar.

To fully describe the operations of this (or any) responsibility center, you must identify the following measures or indicators of performance:

1. *Input Measures*—the resources consumed or costs incurred by the responsibility center.

2. *Workload Measures*—the level of activity or the amount of effort invested in the operations of the responsibility center.

3. *Output Measures*—the amount of goods or services produced or provided by the responsibility center.

4. *Effectiveness Measures*—the extent to which the goals of the responsibility center are achieved. In some responsibility centers (such as production units), effectiveness measures and output measures would be similar (number or value of items produced). In others they may be very different. For example, in a contribution center, sales revenue would be an output measure and monetary contribution to the firm's profits would be an effectiveness measure.

5. *Efficiency Measures*—the ratio of outputs and effectiveness to input and workload measures.

These five types of measures describe the operations of any responsibility center. This framework of types of measures can be applied systematically to ensure an adequate reporting system.

Without this framework, you would have to rely on experience and familiarity with operations to develop general rules regarding appropriate measures. You'd have to depend on guidelines based on experience for such items as production units, keeping track of costs, quality, delivery performance and volume. Often such guidelines are not available, or are not comprehensive. Figure 5 provides you with a list of typical measures for engineered expense centers.

MEASURES FOR DISCRETIONARY EXPENSE CENTERS

Each type of discretionary expense center requires unique measures of performance. Input and workload measures usually pose no problem. But you must carefully choose output and effectiveness measures.

Outputs such as people recruited and trained (personnel), letters,

MEASURES FOR ENGINEERED EXPENSE CENTERS (PRODUCTION UNITS)

Input

Costs
    Direct material
    Direct labor (regular and overtime)
    Overhead
        Indirect labor (regular and overtime)
        Supplies
        Other expenses (utilities, etc.)
    Estimates of inventory (raw material and work-in-process) carrying charges
Resources
    Labor hours
    Machine time
    Inventories (raw material, work-in-process)

Workload

Total number of units worked on (assuming "units" are comparable
Standard cost of work-in-process, rejected work and finished goods (where multiple products are made)

Output

Number of units of finished goods (in single product situations)

Effectiveness

Delivery delays
Backlog of work orders
Rejects, rework (units, money)
Absenteeism
Employee grievances (number/disposition)
Personnel turnover rates
Customer complaints traceable to this responsibility center
Accidents (number, severity indices)

Efficiency

Cost variances
    Materials (price, quantity, yield)
    Labor (rate, efficiency)
    Overhead (controllable, volume)
Idle time
    Labor (by reasons)
    Machines (by causes)
Capacity utilization
Inventories (expressed as days of production)
    raw materials
    work-in-process

Figure 5. A typical list of measures for engineered expense centers

briefs, court cases handled (legal), and new designs, blue-prints (design) may be readily identifiable, but misleading. They contain no indication of quality or timeliness.

Effectiveness measures are important but hard to develop. Often you have to rely on negative indicators of effectiveness, such as complaints from the users of the outputs of these responsibility centers. Figure 6 lists three more centers and the measures common to them.

THE FIRST PRINCIPLE OF MIS DESIGN

The preceding framework suggests the kind of quantitative, routine, internal information that should be part of the MIS. Experience has developed a few vital guiding principles to enhance the effectiveness with which this information is reported and acted upon. You can use the guidelines derived from these principles to assess quickly the quality of your current information system.

The *first principle* is that information-gathering and dissemination should be kept to a minimum. This is desirable for the following two reasons.

1. Information is expensive not only in terms of the time and effort devoted to collection, analysis and presentation, but also in terms of the time wasted by executives on unimportant and trivial information. To the extent that management attention is diverted from the most appropriate priorities, irrelevant or less important information results in great cost to the firm.

2. Information must be kept to a minimum to ensure that managers can fully comprehend what they receive. Human capabilities are limited. The human mind cannot readily absorb and understand large amounts of information. The designer of the MIS must ensure that the outputs of the MIS can be understood and acted upon by the concerned executives.

   Too much information is almost as bad as no information at all. In a large telecommunications organization, the chief executive officer received about three hundred reports from each of fifty geographic units. It was impossible for him to assimilate this mass of information, much less act on it. Everything that the chief executive needed to know was included but was difficult to locate. By employing the techniques explained in this chapter, we were able to eliminate this overload of information on him and reduce it to just one two-page monthly report. Later evaluations of the new MIS were extremely positive. For the first time, the chief executive and other managers in the organization received key information in quantitites that enabled them to identify and remedy problems.

THE SECOND MIS DESIGN PRINCIPLE

The *second guiding principle* is that information contained in formal, routine reports should be tailored to the specific needs of individual recipients. While the needs of each manager are unique, a well-designed MIS will display clearly discernible characteristics. The content and frequency of reports should reflect specific requirements based on the hierarchical level of the managers.

For instance, in General Meters, managers of the lowest level responsibility centers (foundry, machine shop, etc.) would receive reports frequently—daily or weekly—with much detail focusing on physical rather than monetary measures.

Managers at the next level (manufacturing manager, marketing manager) would receive reports less frequently—weekly or monthly— with more aggregated information and greater emphasis on monetary indicators. At the level of the general manager, reports would be prepared monthly or quarterly with even more financial content and less detail.

In a well-designed MIS, the frequency of formal reports should decrease as you go up in the hierarchy. The content also changes with an increasing bias toward financial rather than physical information.

Tailoring information to the needs of the recipient is a demanding exercise, but it reinforces the first principle of MIS design—minimizing the information generated.

THE FINAL MIS PRINCIPLE OF DESIGN

The *third principle* of good MIS design is that "critical variables" and "key result areas" should be explicitly identified and employed in the design of formal reports.

MEASURES FOR REVENUE CENTERS (SALES UNITS)

Input
Units of goods for sale
Marketing expenses
    Salaries
    Commissions
    Distribution, freight
    Advertising, promotion

Workload
Number of calls on customers
Number, weight of units transported
Freight costs

Output
Sales revenue
Units sold
Order backlog
New customers

Effectiveness
Sales revenue
Units sold
Repeat customers
Returns and allowances
Customer complaints
Market share

Efficiency
Marketing expenses as a percent of sales
Receivables expressed as days of sales
Inventories expressed as days of sales
Returns as a percent of sales
Sales ÷ salespersons
Sales ÷ customer
Sales ÷ customer calls

MEASURES FOR CONTRIBUTION CENTERS (MARKETING UNITS)

These would be essentially similar to the measures for revenue centers. The major differences and additions are listed below.

Input — Value of production provided for sale.
Workload — Number or value of quotations, bids made.
Output — Number or value of quotations, bids accepted

Figure 6. A list of measures for several responsibility centers

| *Effectiveness* | Contribution (Sales revenue − Marketing costs − Transfer price of units sold.) |
| *Efficiency* | Orders obtained as a percent of a number and value of quotations, bids made |

MEASURES FOR PROFIT CENTERS (FIRMS AS A WHOLE)

Profit centers usually incorporate expense and revenue/contribution centers. Many measures would be selected from among those already identified for these expense and revenue/contribution centers.

Input	Aggregate of costs incurred by subunit responsibility centers
	Corporate overhead
Workload	Selected measures from individual subunit responsibility centers
Output	Sales revenue
	Units sold (number)
	Order backlog
	Units produced, standard cost of production
	New customers
Effectiveness	Profits (money, growth rate)
	Market share (current, growth rate)
	Personnel/morale
	Absenteeism
	Turnover
	Overtime
	Disputes, Grievances
	Accidents
	Stock price to earnings ratio
	Weighted average cost of capital
	Debt coverage
	Capital expenditure to depreciation ratio
	R&D to discretionary expenses ratio
	Capital projects audit (time and cost to complete)

Figure 6. Continued

The concept of key result areas is based on the fact that the effectiveness of every company and every responsibility center is determined by a critical few of its numerous activities. If you can identify four of five selected indicators or critical variables that reflect how these key activities are being performed, then managers can draw reasonable conclusions about their units' effectiveness.

To illustrate by an example from a familiar industry, the short-term and long-term effectiveness of any hotel can be readily assessed by tracking just two or three critical variables. The room occupancy rate is the most important indicator of short-term profitability. Long-term profitability, especially when competition exists, is influenced by the quality of service. This can be measured by the number and kinds of complaints from guests and the frequency of repeat visits.

In chemical process industries, the yield ratio (output ÷ input) and frequency and duration of breakdowns are the critical variables that adequately describe performance. In most industries, market share is a key overall indicator of effectiveness.

The identification and use of critical variables reinforces the application of the previous two principles. When you use critical variables, you minimize the amount of information needed to describe performance. Also, identification of critical variables ensures that reports are tailored to the characteristics and needs of each responsibility center.

You can employ these three principles not only as a guide to designing an MIS system, but also as a means of assessing the quality of the design of existing information systems. If the design of the existing MIS does not reflect the application of these principles, then a careful and comprehensive re-design should be considered.

Besides these guiding principles, there are a few important technical considerations that can greatly improve the value of the MIS for planning and control.

THE MULTIPLE DIMENSIONS OF INFORMATION

Each piece of information that is part of an MIS can possess several dimensions. Both designers and users of the MIS must be very much aware of this fact. You can look at the same item of information in many ways. Consider this example.

In GMC, an expense of $1,000 was incurred. The amount of the expense is one dimension of the information. Suppose the expense was incurred by and included in the report of the responsibility center headed by the product manager-industrial products. The information now possesses two dimensions, the amount and the responsibility center that incurred this expense.

The report may also indicate that the $1,000 was spent on travel. The traveling may have been done by the salesperson operating on the west coast. You now have three further dimensions—the purpose of incurring the expense, the geographic area in which it was incurred, and the level of the person incurring the expense. A sixth dimension would be the time period, the month in which the expense was incurred. The type of customer being contacted could be a seventh dimension. And so on.

The illustration suggests that the number and types of dimensions for any one piece of information is dependent on the kind of analyses needed to manage the responsibility center effectively. The manager of the responsibility center and the designer of the MIS need to determine in advance what dimensions are important and should be recorded.

If several dimensions are important, you should consider the use of electronic data processing to facilitate the coding, retrieval and analysis of the various dimensions.

TIMELINESS VS. ACCURACY

One commonly encountered decision in the design of the MIS is the choice between timeliness and accuracy of information. It is often possible to get an approximation of the actual figures on performance before you obtain final, accurate, legally acceptable figures.

In general, if there is a question as to which figures you will use in an MIS—approximate, speedily obtained information or accurate, delayed information—opt for the approximate, timely information.

For example, from a managerial standpoint, obtaining approximate financial statements within a week after the close of an accounting period is much more useful than getting accurate statements that will satisfy an external auditor two months later.

Treating dispatches from warehouses as equivalent to sales may be appropriate when designing an MIS for a high volume, low margin business, though traditional accountants would consider such a practice unacceptable. Estimations of changes in work-in-process may be unnecessary for production units where such work is either stable or small. In those production units, tracking finished goods alone would be an entirely satisfactory estimate of workload or output for a manager.

EARLY WARNING INDICATORS

Most information systems record historical performance. The concept of leading indicators, which has been widely accepted and used in the context of macro-economics, has received little attention in the context of the performance of individual firms.

For instance, monitoring employee grievances and absenteeism may enable managers to recognize and remedy morale problems that otherwise might result in debilitating rates of turnover in personnel. Age analyses of accounts receivable might signal emerging cash flow problems before they actually occur. Analyzing increases in customer complaints may reveal quality or design problems that could have caused severe profit problems if they were not immediately rectified.

TRACKING TRENDS

Information about the performance of a responsibility center at a particular point in time or for a single accounting period is valuable. However, information about trends in performance greatly facilitates managerial planning and control.

Keeping track of performance over several reporting periods enables managers to readily identify causes of good and poor performance. Also, they can forecast future performance more reliably and accurately if records of past trends are available.

The importance of recording trends cannot be overstated. Random events will inevitably influence performance. To react to every deviation in performance is counter-productive. But you must not ignore a two or three-month trend that indicates a continuing, identifiable, non-random problem.

Information reports should contain data not only about the im-

It is possible to identify potential problems and make sure they don't occur if the system is well designed. A subsidiary of a multinational pharmaceutical firm formerly based its marketing and sales reports on an analysis of invoices. Sales in April would be analyzed in May and suitable managerial action would be taken to correct problems that had occurred in April.

This practice was typical of most firms in the industry. We changed it when we re-designed its MIS. The new marketing and sales reports included analyses based on indents (requisitions) from the firm's distributors. These indents were received twice monthly, by the 5th and 20th of each month. Production schedules were developed based on these indents and goods were dispatched by the 15th and 30th day of each month.

With the introduction of the new reports based on the indents received in, for example, April, the marketing manager could compare the volume indented by the fifth to the planned sales for the month of April. He then took actions in the month of April itself that would influence the second indent received in that month.

The medical representatives (salesmen) in each territory were informed of the products they were expected to emphasize. Sometimes product promotions or discounts were speedily initiated to influence the second set of indents in the month. Thus, by means of a simple change in the MIS, the marketing manager was able to take actions in the same month to remedy shortcomings. This would have been impossible to do under the old system, which permitted action only in the month of May, *after* the problems in April had already occurred.

mediately past period, but also year-to-date performance. An even better approach is to include information about the past 12 months; updated in each report on a rolling basis.

FORMAT DESIGN: THE SINGLE REPORT APPROACH

The design of the format in which you make reports merits attention. It is very useful to attempt to provide all the information pertaining to a responsibility center in just one page or at least in a single report.

There are two important reasons why there should be a single report incorporating all the indicators of performance for a reporting period, rather than several reports received at various points in time.

The first reason is that the endeavor to include all relevant information in a single report, preferably consisting of a single page, would demand the principles of good design—identification of critical variables, tailoring information to the recipients' needs, and minimizing the information provided.

The second and more important reason is that providing all relevant indicators of performance in a single report greatly facilitates comprehension and integration of the pieces of information by the recipient.

For instance, at GMC the overtime figures in hours and dollars are important to the foreman of the assembly shop. If the foreman also receives absenteeism figures simultaneously, he can then assess the extent to which unexpected absenteeism affected the overtime figure.

Furthermore, if the level of activity or workload figures are also provided at the same time, each item of information takes on significantly greater meaning than would any one item alone.

The foreman, receiving all three items of information simultaneously, can analyze the extent to which overtime wages have resulted from worker absenteeism, from the workload and from inefficiency. Appropriate remedial action can then be more reliably identified and taken.

Providing comprehensive information in a single report makes it possible to gain an overall, integrated view of the operations of a responsibility center.

One disadvantage of employing a single report is that the workload of the department running the MIS would be very great at particular points of time. If indicators of performance are split into groups and provided by means of staggered reports generated at various points in time, the workload of the MIS department or personnel would be more stable. You should weigh the advantages of a single report against this disadvantage.

FINANCIAL AND PHYSICAL INFORMATION

In designing the format of the report, it is extremely useful to separate financial and physical indicators of performance.

Every item of financial information in the firm necessarily has to be linked. For instance, the salaries and wages of the responsibility centers under the marketing manager must be added to those incurred by the responsibility centers under the manufacturing manager, the chief accountant and the personnel manager to obtain the salaries and wages of all personnel reporting to the general manager of GMC. Similarly, other items of costs and revenue need to be linked in order to obtain the financial picture for GMC as a whole.

In contrast to financial information, physical indicators of performance tend to be relevant to only one or two levels in the firm's hierarchy and to individual functional areas such as marketing or personnel. The number of distributors visited by the salesmen reporting to the product manager-residential products is not of much value to the general manager. The manufacturing manager would find such information entirely irrelevant.

EXCEPTION REPORTING

The "exception principle" or "management by exception" is fundamental to the effective use of an MIS. Essentially, management by exception means that only occurrences that merit managerial concern and actions are brought to the attention of managers.

In order to identify exceptions, you must first identify the standard or normal expectation.

The exception principle requires that your reporting formats identify the difference or variance between these standards-expectations-budgets and actual performance. By scanning these variances, a manager can identify which activities or operations require further analysis and remedial action.

In order to minimize the number of columns in the report, all three pieces of information (actual, budget and variance) are not necessary. Experience indicates that the actual and variance information are sufficient.

ROUTING THE REPORTS

It is not uncommon for managers to request that reports going to all their subordinates go to them also. The general manager at GMC, for example, might ask that all reports intended for the foremen and product managers be provided to him. The problem of information overload is likely to occur under such circumstances.

The better practice is that each manager receives the report specifically designed for him *and* the reports intended for managers reporting directly to him. The general manager at GMC should get his report and the reports intended for the manufacturing manager, marketing manager, chief accountant and personnel manager. The manufacturing manager would get his report and the reports going to the foremen.

This practice reduces the likelihood of information overload. It also recognizes the reality that managers often require more detail about particular aspects of the operations in their charge. Thus, the general manager would have the marketing manager's report if there are more details about the marketing operations that he might want to know in a particular reporting period.

The likelihood of the general manager needing the detail in the reports going to the product managers is remote, however. The marketing manager is the best source for such details. To provide the product managers' reports to the general manager would therefore be unnecessary, if not undesirable.

EXAMPLES OF REPORTS

Figures 7 and 8 illustrate the principles and techniques of design presented in this chapter. They are examples of forms that could be used at GMC. Reporting forms for the manufacturing manager (Figure 7) and the product manager-industrial products (Figure 8) show the detailed requirements for different hierarchical levels and functional areas.

ACTION REQUIREMENTS

If your firm already has an MIS, collect sample reports for each of the responsibility centers that you identified at the end of the previous Section. The sample reports should be filled in, rather than left blank. Blank reports will not provide an understanding of what information is actually being provided and what is desired but not currently generated.

Evaluate the reports using the three basic principles mentioned

GMC: PERFORMANCE REPORT FOR MANUFACTURING MANAGER

MONTH: YEAR:

	TOTAL MANUFACTURING				FOUNDRY				MACHINE SHOP				ASSEMBLY				MAINTENANCE			
FINANCIAL PERFORMANCE	YEAR TO DATE		CURRENT PERIOD		YEAR TO DATE		CURRENT PERIOD		YEAR TO DATE		CURRENT PERIOD		YEAR TO DATE		CURRENT PERIOD		YEAR TO DATE		CURRENT PERIOD	
($x000)	ACTUAL	VARIANCE	ACTUAL	VARIANCE	ACT.	VAR.	ACT.	VAR.	ACT.	VAR.	ACT.	VAR.	ACT.	VAR.	ACT.	VAR.	ACT.	VAR.	ACT.	VAR.
LABOR COMPENSATION																				
LABOR-RELATED BENEFITS																				
RAW MATERIAL CONSUMPTION																				
SUPPLIES & SMALL TOOLS																				
UTILITIES																				
OTHER OPERATING EXPENSE																				
TOTAL MFG. EXPENSES																				
OPERATIONAL (PHYSICAL) INDICATORS																				
HEAD COUNT — DIRECT																				
HEAD COUNT — INDIRECT																				
HEAD COUNT — TOTAL																				
CAPACITY UTILIZATION (%)																				
ABSENTEEISM (%)																				
OVERTIME — $																				
OVERTIME — HOURS																				
DOWN-TIME — BREAK-DOWNS																				
DOWN-TIME — LACK OF OPERATOR																				
DOWN-TIME — LACK OF R.M.																				
DOWN-TIME — TOTAL																				
ACCIDENTS #																				
SEVERITY																				
GRIEVANCES INITIATED																				
WORK-IN-PROCESS INVENTORY																				
RAW MATERIAL INVENTORY																				
PRODUCTION VOLUME																				

Copy to: General Manager

Figure 7. A typical performance report for a manufacturing manager

FINANCIAL PERFORMANCE	YEAR TO DATE TOTAL		TOTAL		PRODUCT TYPE 1		PRODUCT TYPE 2		OTHER PRODUCT TYPES	
	ACTUAL	VARIANCE	ACTUAL	VARIANCE	ACTUAL	VARIANCE	ACTUAL	VARIANCE	ACTUAL	VARIANCE
NORTH-EAST REGION										
REVENUE										
TRANSFER PRICE OF GOODS SOLD										
CONTRIBUTION MARGIN										
RELATED REGIONAL EXPENSES										
ADJUSTED REGIONAL CONTRBN. MARGIN										
MID-WEST REGION										
REVENUE										
TRANSFER PRICE OF GOODS SOLD										
CONTRIBUTION MARGIN										
RELATED REGIONAL EXPENSES										
ADJUSTED REGIONAL CONTRBN. MARGIN										
WEST REGION										
REVENUE										
TRANSFER PRICE OF GOODS SOLD										
CONTRIBUTION MARGIN										
RELATED REGIONAL EXPENSES										
ADJUSTED REGIONAL CONTRBN. MARGIN										
SOUTH-WEST REGION										
REVENUE										
TRANSFER PRICE OF GOODS SOLD										
CONTRIBUTION MARGIN										
RELATED REGIONAL EXPENSES										
ADJUSTED REGIONAL CONTRBN. MARGIN										
TOTAL REGIONAL CONTRIBUTION MARGIN										
PRODUCT MANAGER'S OVERHEAD										
CONTRIBUTION BEFORE MARKETING AND CORPORATE OVERHEADS										

NEXT MONTH REVENUE FORECAST

N.E.	
M-W.	
W.	
S.W.	
TOTAL	

Copy to: Marketing Manager

Figure 8. A typical performance report for a product manager—industrial products

SALES PERFORMANCE

SALES PERFORMANCE		YEAR TO DATE		CURRENT PERIOD	
		ACTUAL	VARIANCE	ACTUAL	VARIANCE
Order Backlog	N.E.				
	M-W.				
	W.				
	S.W.				
	TOTAL				
No. of Employees	N.E.				
	M-W.				
	W.				
	S.W.				
	TOTAL				

ACCOUNTS RECEIVABLE ANALYSIS

AGE	TOTAL	N.E.	M-W.	W.	S.W.
<31 days					
31-45 days					
46-60 days					
>60 days					
TOTAL					
ACTUAL					
VARIANCE					

DISTRIBUTION PERFORMANCE

INDICATORS	YEAR TO DATE AVERAGE		CURRENT PERIOD	
	ACTUAL	VARIANCE	ACTUAL	VARIANCE
Total Freight Expenses ($)				
Delivery Delays (#)				
Delivery Delays ($)				
Freight as % of Sales Value				

SALES PERFORMANCE

SALES PERFORMANCE		YEAR TO DATE		CURRENT PERIOD	
		ACTUAL	VARIANCE	ACTUAL	VARIANCE
Calls Per Sales-Person	N.E.				
	M-W.				
	W.				
	S.W.				
	TOTAL				
Selling Expenses to Sales Ratio	N.E.				
	M-W.				
	W.				
	S.W.				
	TOTAL				
Contribution Margin to Sales (%)	N.E.				
	M-W.				
	W.				
	S.W.				
	TOTAL				
Contribution Margin Variance Due to Product Mix ($)	N.E.				
	M-W.				
	W.				
	S.W.				
	TOTAL				
Contribution Margin Variance Due to Price Change ($)	N.E.				
	M-W.				
	W.				
	S.W.				
	TOTAL				
Contribution Margin Variance Due to Volume ($)	N.E.				
	M-W.				
	W.				
	S.W.				
	TOTAL				
Orders Booked	N.E.				
	M-W.				
	W.				
	S.W.				
	TOTAL				

N.E. - Northeast
M-W. - Midwest
W. - West
S.W. - Southwest

Figure 8. Continued

in this chapter. Is the information excessive? Are the reports tailored (in content and frequency) to the needs of the individual recipients? Are the critical variables identified?

If your evaluation is negative or you do not already have a formal MIS in operation, you'll need to identify the input, workload, output, effectiveness and efficiency measures for each of the responsibility centers. Work closely with the managers of the responsibility centers in selecting the relevant measures and identifying the critical variables. The approach to employ is discussed in detail in Section XII which focuses on implementing the new system.

After developing a preliminary definition of the information needs of each responsibility center, you must design a reporting format that incorporates this information. The ideal guidelines for designing reporting formats include:

1. Employing the single report approach
2. Recognizing the multiple dimensions of information
3. Providing information on trends
4. Separating financial and physical indicators
5. Utilizing the principle of exception reporting
6. Specifying the two recipients of each report

Test these reports out using the data from historical records. You may find that some of the information you need is not currently being recorded. Make arrangements to record such information in the future. Also, at this time you may have to make compromises on the accuracy of the information that you use in order to ensure its timely availability.

Discuss the new reports with each recipient and modify them if you are convinced that changes are necessary. Then conduct a trial run of the new system to obtain further feedback from the users.

Do not eliminate any existing reports until you are absolutely confident that you have the data base and the resources (personnel and equipment) in place and functioning for the new system. This means a period of very high workloads for the MIS department.

At this stage, you may be unable to calculate variances. You may not have developed the standards, expectations and budgets necessary to provide the benchmarks against which actual performance should be compared. The development of these benchmarks is the next step toward the new system of budgeting for profit.

IV

Setting Standards Within Responsibility Centers

The first step toward specifying the benchmarks against which you will assess actual performance is to set standards for discrete operations or individual activities within responsibility centers. These activities or operations should a) be repetitive in nature; and b) possess clearly identifiable inputs and outputs. The process of converting inputs to outputs does not need to be well-defined.

ANALYZING TARGET OPERATIONS

Activities with clearly identifiable inputs and outputs normally occur in engineered expense centers. The foundry, machine shop and assembly operations at GMC are examples of situations where formal standards can and should be specified.

In the foundry, the output in terms of number of units obtained from a given weight of inputs would be a useful standard. The time needed to carry out various machining or assembly operations in the other two engineered expense centers would similarly constitute a useful set of standards.

You will find repetitive activities with clearly defined inputs and outputs in other types of responsibility centers too. For instance, in a maintenance shop, you can develop standards that specify the time within which specific preventive maintenance activities should be accomplished.

Standards can be set for the time and cost of supplies for breakdown maintenance activities that occur frequently. In rayon spinning plants, for example, the electric motors that operate the spinning machines frequently break down because of the acids employed in the processs. The time required to replace a motor can and should be specified in this situation.

Numerous other standards are commonly used in both manufacturing and service businesses, including:

- invoices handled per hour
- customer service calls per day
- rejects on an assembly line
- product defects uncovered per thousand
- customer complaints resolved per employee
- parts inspected per hour.

In revenue centers and contribution centers, the "pre-sale" operations involving customer relations, product specification, and preparing quotations *are not* suitable activities for developing standards. The "post-sale" operations involving packaging, freight and other distribution-related activities *are* situations where setting a standard is desirable.

You need to exercise careful judgment in discretionary expense centers. Certain activities might be repetitive enough and important enough to justify setting standards for them. For example, standards may be appropriate in personnel's preliminary screening of applications for entry-level positions. But the same department's handling of grievances is not readily susceptible to time standards. Similarly, it would be meaningless to specify the briefs per man-day you want your legal department to generate.

WHY DEVELOP STANDARDS?

It is not uncommon to hear managers argue that the development of formally stated standards of performance for individual activities within responsibility centers is unnecessary. One plant manager working in a process industry told us:

> "... I am not really convinced of the need for standards. Just by walking through the plant, I can very easily tell whether everything is running as it should or not. Why go through all this trouble when really it is unnecessary and unlikely to improve the performance of the plant?"

You should consider identifying some of the following benefits of formal standards to develop an understanding of how important standards are to both your individual firm and its managers.

1. Formal standards contribute to the elimination of implicit, subjective, often unconscious biases. If the expected level of performance is formally and explicity recorded and communicated, then it also must be justifiable. Consequently, you can more readily identify and correct any subjective and unjustifiable expectations of individual managers.

2. Formal standards contribute to the continuity of knowledge in the firm. An experienced manager might understand what is acceptable performance for various activities in his responsibility center. But your firm would lose that knowledge if the manager leaves or is promoted or transferred, unless a written record of the standards exists.

   Some managers consciously avoid records of their operations to make themselves indispensable to the firm. Formal performance standards and records minimize these problems and promote that continuity of knowledge.

3. Formal standards of performance are an important means of communication within the firm. They reflect a common understanding among levels in the hierarchy of what constitutes acceptable performance. Standards also facilitate communication between interdependent departments such as sales and distribution, or production and purchasing.

4. Standards are essential if you want to practice "management by exception." You can't identify or highlight deviations from expected performance unless a clear understanding exists of what constitutes standard performance.

5. Formal standards facilitate the analysis of trends in performance. A manager may be able to assess how well a particular operation or acitivity is working at a specific point in time without formal standards. But in order to assess cumulative performance over a long period, formal records and standards are essential.

6. You can employ formal standards as a motivational device. Standards that are relatively hard to achieve may stimulate greater efforts by your workers. Or you may consciously set standards at a lower level to encourage new workers.

7. Standards are of great value for planning, in addition to control. Standards of material usage and output per worker-hour, for instance, greatly assist the planning of materials purchases and worker recruitment and training.

CHARACTERISTICS OF ACCEPTABLE STANDARDS

Based on an assessment of the benefits expected from setting standards, you identify and select certain activities within each of the responsibility centers for setting standards.

Before selecting the appropriate techniques for setting these standards you should recognize what makes a standard acceptable to the concerned personnel.

We cannot overemphasize the importance of standards being acceptable to the personnel involved. A standard that is not accepted by the individual performing the activity and by his superior is even less desirable than having no standard at all. An unaccepted standard contributes to an erosion of commitment and motivation, leads to frequent disagreements and detracts from the quality of managerial decision-making.

A standard that is not accepted by the individual performing the activity and by his superior is even less desirable than having no standard at all. An unaccepted standard contributes to an erosion of commitment and motivation, leads to frequent disagreements and detracts from the quality of managerial decision-making.

Table 3 reveals one executive's opinion on the necessity of an employee-oriented attitude toward standards.

The single most important characteristic that leads to acceptance of a standard of performance is that it is *perceived as fair and reasonable*.

"You must remember two things about developing perform-ance standards," claims a widely-respected former treasurer and chief financial officer. "The first is that they are definitely an integral part of any modern company's control and productivity improvement efforts.

"The second is often overlooked, but just as important. You can't just concentrate on the benefits of such systems to the company. Without worker and manager compliance, you have nothing. Explain how they will benefit. It takes time and education.

"The initial introduction is the hardest. Most managers think they are sharp enough to know what's going on without stan-dards. The employees love that attitude. You don't think they can fool your managers?

"What's a normal-looking level of scrap on the floor? One inch or 1.2 inches? Can you tell the difference? If the lathe oper-ator thinks you can, don't you think he can spread it around a little?

"Walking through a plant, can you tell whether there are 44 parts at a work station that should only have 40? Is a person reading a blueprint goofing off because he doesn't want to start another lot 20 minutes before quitting time?

"Whatever you do in the way of standard-setting, make sure that you also stay aware of the human aspects of the changes from both the workers' and the managers' viewpoints."

Table 3. An executive's assessment of the need for standards

Unfortunately, the understanding of what is fair and reasonable varies according to the audience. Top management might consider a standard fair and reasonable if it is as close as possible to ideal per-formance. Those being evaluated on the basis of the standard might consider a standard fair and reasonable if it appears to be easily attainable.

Reconciling these two points of view is a difficult task. Any tech-nique that is chosen to develop standards should be applied with sen-sitivity. You must recognize the need to arrive at a reasoned compromise between the conflicting expectations of superiors and subordinates.

CLASSIFYING STANDARD-SETTING TECHNIQUES

The number of possible techniques for developing standards is limited only by human ingenuity. Essentially, a technique is a method to arrive at an acceptable understanding of the relationships between inputs and outputs that would exist under normal conditions, when an operation or activity is carried out efficiently and with a satisfactory degree of effectiveness.

The phrase "normal conditions" recognizes the resource limitations and other constraints that make actual performance less than the ideal. The relationships between inputs and outputs would not represent ideal performance. Nor would they necessarily reflect the lowest acceptable level of performance. They *would* represent performance that requires a reasonable amount of effort and motivation on the part of the subordinates.

The numerous techniques for developing standards are generally classified in three categories. Each of these categories possesses advantages and disadvantages which make them desirable or undesirable in specific situations:

1. theoretical and engineered approaches;
2. historical and statistical approaches; and
3. comparative and subjective approaches.

THEORETICAL AND ENGINEERED APPROACHES

These approaches assume that you can calculate optimal input-output relationships. Some differences exist between the theoretical approach and the engineered approach. An example of a standard developed by the theoretical approach would be the output per hour of a machine, based on the manufacturer's specifications. The theoretical approach is based on machine or process specifications.

The engineered approach, on the other hand, is applicable to situations where human physical endeavors determine ouput. This approach is based on industrial engineering techniques, such as time and motion studies.

The engineered approach has several disadvantages. First, it is expensive and time-consuming. Second, it demands special technical expertise from the individual specifying the standard. Third, and most important, the individuals evaluated on the basis of engineered standards usually do not readily accept either the process of arriving at those standards or the actual standards themselves.

Engineered standards are often arrived at without the workers' involvement and are consequently viewed with suspicion. This is particularly unfortunate since this approach is applicable to situations where human endeavor primarily determines the level of ouput.

In certain situations where an atmosphere of trust and cooperation exists, engineered standards, or a combination of engineered and theoretical standards, becomes appropriate. For instance, in the communications industry, the cost of making cable joints can be analyzed in terms of the materials (theoretical) and man-hours (engineered) required. A standard is then arrived at for the cost of "jointing" cables of various sizes.

HISTORICAL AND STATISTICAL APPROACHES

These approaches apply in situations where you cannot specify input-output relationships on the basis of theoretical and engineered approaches, or where theoretical and engineered approaches are unlikely to find acceptance. Such approaches assume that you have historical records of past performance.

The historical approach relies on the projection of trends in past performance to arrive at an understanding of an acceptable current standard. Usually an arbitrary 5% to 10% improvement over past performance is also incorporated.

This approach has the obvious limitation that, unless past performance approximates optimal performance, past inefficiencies may be treated as acceptable. Also, an arbitrary determination of desired improvements in performance is likely to have a demotivating effect.

The statistical approach to developing standards can be considerably more sophisticated than the historical approach. The well-known statistical quality control technique of setting "control limits" for a process can be usefully applied to the development of standards in operations where there are considerable variations in performance due to more than one cause.

For example, you could use this method to develop standards of consumption for stores' items, spares and accessories consumed in an irregular fashion. Assume first that variations in consumption are primarily due to (i) chance causes, (ii) quality of the items being consumed and (iii) assignable causes independent of the first two. Then assume that variation due to chance causes is so intractable that the difference between the savings arising out of their identification and the cost of identifying those causes would be insignificant or negative.

It is then a simple matter, if enough data is available, to statistically determine the limits within which consumption would fall if there were no variations in quality. If consumption figures for an item fall outside the determined limits, then you can presume with a calculable degree of confidence that the quality of the item is at fault.

---

a. Examine thoroughly the relevant records containing the data for the immediately previous year to clearly identify cases of abnormally good or bad performance. Ascertain the reasons for such abnormal performance. When due to uncontrollable factors (like machine malfunction, breakdowns, unusually poor or good quality of raw material or processing material, excessive loads arising out of rush orders, etc.), exclude these readings for the purpose of determining standards.

b. After you eliminate the abnormal readings, sort out the remaining readings according to the level of performance achieved, beginning from the highest level of performance downwards.

c. Plot the distribution indicated by the first thirty readings in this prioritized list (or a number of readings representing not less than 15% of the total sample).

d. If you are specifying *range* of acceptable performance, then the highest and lowest readings now remaining would define this standard range.

e. If you are specifying a *single value* that represents acceptable performance, then the average of the remaining readings would be the standard.

Table 4. A five-step process for statistical analysis

ANOTHER STATISTICAL METHOD

Another "statistical" method of developing standards, which is extremely useful in practice and which has several advantageous characteristics, is described in Table 4. This method is successful in responding to the basic problems encountered in specifying standards.

STATISTICAL STANDARDS IN ACTION

Figure 9 presents the readings relating to the consumption in the foundry of GMC of a fluxing agent (Chemical A) that is added to the molten metal to give the castings certain desired characteristics. Both the consumption of Chemical A and the output (castings) are specified in kilograms.

In order to arrive at the data presented in Figure 9, the 450 readings of the relationship between the consumption of Chemical A and output that were taken over the past year were scanned to identify abnormal readings. Only 17 readings were found to be abnormal, leaving 433. These 433 readings were then ranked and the top 65 (15% of 433) readings are listed in Figure 9.

In Figure 10, these 65 readings are regrouped into eighteen categories. This is an arbitrary number. But in order to get an understanding of how these readings are distributed, we have found it useful to work with 15 to 20 groups of readings if there are large numbers of readings involved.

The average reading is 0.004638. This could serve as the standard. Alternatively, if the standard is to be specified in terms of upper and lower limits of acceptable performance, these limits could be 0.00156 to 0.01003 (from Figure 9, readings ranked 1 and 65).

The advantage of plotting the readings as shown in Figure 10 is that you can get a visual understanding of past performance. Looking at Figure 10 you might decide that instead of using the average reading as the standard, the large number of readings falling within the group 0.00450 to 0.00500 indicates you should establish the standard as the mid-point of this group, i.e., 0.00475. Alternatively, if you are determining a range of acceptable readings, you could specify this range as 0.0030 to 0.00550 because 49 of the 65 readings fall within this range.

"STATISTICAL" METHOD OF DEVELOPING STANDARDS

Table of 65 (15%) Best Readings Out of 433 Normal Readings Selected From 450 Readings

Ratio of Chemical A: Output

Sl. NO.	TOTAL OUTPUT (KGS)	CHEMICAL CON-SUMPTION (KGS)	RATIO	RANK	Sl. NO.	TOTAL OUTPUT (KGS)	CHEMICAL CON-SUMPTION (KGS)	RATIO	RANK
1.	809.8	3.0	0.00370	13	34.	460.2	4.5	0.00978	64
2.	611.3	2.5	0.00409	18	35.	722.5	4.0	0.00554	56
3.	615.0	2.5	0.00407	17	36.	687.5	3.5	0.00509	49
4.	945.4	3.0	0.00317	7	37.	776.7	3.5	0.00451	30
5.	746.3	3.0	0.00402	15	38.	484.3	2.0	0.00413	19
6.	653.6	3.0	0.00459	33	39.	588.5	2.5	0.00425	24
7.	745.1	1.5	0.00201	3	40.	556.6	2.0	0.00359	12
8.	827.3	3.5	0.00423	23	41.	622.6	3.0	0.00482	41
9.	1076.8	3.0	0.00279	6	42.	751.4	4.0	0.00532	54
10.	605.2	2.5	0.00413	20	43.	677.2	3.0	0.00443	25
11.	725.9	3.5	0.00482	40	44.	592.3	3.0	0.00507	48
12.	783.2	3.5	0.00447	27	45.	633.8	3.0	0.00473	38
13.	805.5	3.0	0.00372	14	46.	628.7	4.0	0.00636	58
14.	721.6	3.0	0.00416	21	47.	646.4	4.5	0.00696	61

No.				No.			
15.	641.8	1.0	0.00156	**1**			
16.	615.4	3.0	0.00487	44			
17.	868.7	3.0	0.00345	9			
18.	867.6	3.0	0.00346	10			
19.	629.1	1.5	0.00238	5			
20.	660.7	3.0	0.00454	32			
21.	652.0	3.0	0.00460	34			
22.	470.6	2.5	0.00531	53			
23.	477.4	2.0	0.00419	22			
24.	482.6	4.0	0.00933	63			
25.	664.4	4.5	0.00677	59			
26.	530.7	4.0	0.00754	62			
27.	704.0	3.5	0.00497	46			
28.	538.8	2.5	0.00464	35			
29.	688.7	1.5	0.00218	4			
30.	505.5	1.0	0.00198	2			
31.	629.2	3.0	0.00477	39			
32.	577.6	3.0	0.00519	50			
33.	620.7	2.5	0.00403	16			
48.	659.1	4.5	0.00683	60			
49.	797.6	8.0	0.01003	65			
50.	910.7	3.0	0.00329	8			
51.	1049.9	5.5	0.00524	51			
52.	637.3	3.0	0.00471	37			
53.	783.2	3.5	0.00446	26			
54.	892.7	4.0	0.00440	29			
55.	559.7	2.5	0.00447	28			
56.	722.5	2.5	0.00346	11			
57.	638.0	3.0	0.00470	36			
58.	993.3	4.5	0.00453	31			
59.	719.5	3.5	0.00486	43			
60.	719.5	3.5	0.00486	42			
61.	709.5	3.5	0.00493	45			
62.	800.8	4.0	0.00500	47			
63.	761.9	4.0	0.00525	52			
64.	708.1	4.0	0.00565	57			
65.	831.0	4.5	0.00542	55			
Total	45168.5	209.5	0.004638				

Figure 9. Table of readings for statistical development of standards

Chemical A: Output

FREQUENCY DISTRIBUTION OF 65 BEST READINGS

0.00151	-	0.00200	//
0.00201	-	0.00250	///
0.00251	-	0.00300	/
0.00301	-	0.00350	~~////~~
0.00351	-	0.00400	///
0.00401	-	0.00450	~~////~~ ~~////~~ //
0.00451	-	0.00500	~~////~~ ~~////~~ ~~////~~ ~~////~~ /
0.00501	-	0.00550	~~////~~ ///
0.00551	-	0.00600	//
0.00601	-	0.00650	/
0.00651	-	0.00700	///
0.00701	-	0.00750	
0.00751	-	0.00800	/
0.00801	-	0.00850	
0.00851	-	0.00900	
0.00901	-	0.00950	/
0.00951	-	0.01000	/
Above 0.01000			/
			65 Readings

Average Reading = 0.004638

Range of Readings = 0.00156 - 0.01003

Figure 10. A useful grouping for frequency distribution

The advantages of this method are:

i. it is much less expensive and time-consuming than approaches based on time and motion studies;

ii. the standard you arrive at would represent a level of performance which had actually been achieved in the past. It would therefore be acceptable from the point of view of feasibility of attainment;

iii. at the same time, it would represent a level of performance distinctly higher than past average performance and would therefore be acceptable in terms of improvement in performance;

iv. once the method is explained and understood, you could generate a feeling of participation on the part of individuals to be evaluated by having them develop the standard themselves; and

v. over a period of time, if actual performance meets the standard specified and the standard is revised, then performance should gradually approach the optimal level.

There are certain disadvantages inherent in this method. If management control is lax and performance is allowed to deteriorate, the standard, when reviewed, would also fall. In addition, the method has no real statistical justification. It needs to be appreciated purely as a mechanism for arriving at an *acceptable* standard, which would be independent of the person employing the method.

The suggestion, in step "c" of Table 4, that you not select less than the best 15% of the normal readings is important. If you take less than 15% of the best readings, the standard arrived at would represent a relatively higher level of performance, and if more than 15% are taken the standard will be lowered.

If fact, if 100% of the normal readings are taken, then the standard you arrive at would represent the *average* performance in the period. While that suggested figure of 15% is arbitrary, we have found that it often represents a level of performance that demands extra effort from subordinates and yet, at the same time, is not so high as to be discouraging.

COMPARATIVE AND SUBJECTIVE APPROACHES

These approaches are useful only in those situations where you cannot apply theoretical, engineered, statistical and historical approaches. The comparative approach assumes that the operation or activity for which you are developing standards is identical or very similar to operations or activities being performed in other locations or organizations.

You presume that the standards set in those other situations are applicable to the operation or activity under study. The limitations of this approach are obvious.

The subjective approach, as the name suggests, is essentially a judgmental, managerial assessment of what the standard should be.

Both these approaches, while possessing limitations, do have their uses. For example, firms in developing countries have used the comparative approach when initially setting up industries which have been in existence in more developed countries for substantial periods of time.

The subjective approach is valuable in situations where managerial decisions must be made about matters such as the level and quality of service to be provided to customers for competitive purposes. An organization such as an airline might make a decision that any phone call from a potential customer should be responded to within 20 seconds in order to ensure that the customer does not go to a competitive airline. Such a standard, while undoubtedly subjective and perhaps arbitrary, is still valuable because it represents an assessment of the level of service that should be provided in order to remain in business.

ACTION REQUIREMENTS

For each of the responsibility centers identified at the end of Section II, analyze the operations and locate those activites that are repetitive in nature and have well-defined inputs and outputs. In particular, scan the reports that emerged from Section III to identify the activites that are critical to the performance of those responsibility centers.

You will have to develop standards for those activities included in the reports. For the activities not included, you will have to judge whether the benefits of formal standards justify the time and effort to develop and update them.

If theoretical and engineered approaches are practical, inexpensive and acceptable to those concerned, use those methods to develop standards. If these methods are impractical, expensive or unacceptable, the statistical method is the next best alternative. If historical records are unavailable or competitive pressures are extreme, comparative and subjective approaches may be appropriate.

It is important to remember that the techniques discussed in this Section are applicable only to *activities within responsibility centers*. In order to specify the expected performance of a responsibility center as a whole, or the overall profit performance of a firm, you'll need more complex methods. These are discussed in the following sections.

V

Developing the
Production Budget

The performance reports for the responsibility centers that carry out the production function are a good place to start to design the production budget. These performance reports identify the critical areas where expectations regarding satisfactory performance must be stated.

For the important individual activities within the responsibility centers, standards should be set based on the methods suggested in Section IV. For the responsibility center as a whole—particularly with regard to aggregate financial performance—such standard-setting techniques would be inappropriate.

PERFORMANCE FACTORS TO CONSIDER

In order to budget for expected performance, you must consider the impact of several sets of factors.

First, review the *past performance* of the responsibility center.

Second, recognize that factors *external* to the responsibility center may significantly influence performance. For instance, a shortage of skilled machinists could affect the performance capabilities of the machine shop at General Meters Corporation.

Third, remember that the amount and kind of *resources* being made available to the responsibility center can affect performance. If extra lathes or milling machines are added to the machine shop, its aggregate performance capabilities will increase.

Fourth, in describing aggregate performance of a responsibility center, consider the impact of normal *seasonal changes* on demand for the end-products. Aggregate performance in the winter months, when housing starts are reduced, would be different for GMC's residential meters when compared to the peak activity periods in the spring and summer months.

Fifth, realize that aggregate performance is affected by the detailed *plans of action* adopted by the managers of the various responsibility centers. The foreman of the assembly shop may decide to adopt new scheduling practices during the coming budget period. Or additions to the work force may be scheduled at different times than in the past.

The response to seasonal changes in the level of activity could level the workload by building the inventories of residential meters in the winter months. The usual lead time between receiving a special order for an industrial meter and making the delivery could perhaps be reduced by increasing the number of items stored in the raw materials inventories—and so on.

Finally, you need to make sure the production budget is *flexible* enough to recognize the impact on performance of varying levels of activity caused by factors other than just seasonal considerations.

DESIGNING THE PRODUCTION BUDGET FORMAT

The design of the production budget is not as complex as it might first appear, if you have already designed performance reports. Figure 11 uses the machine shop at GMC to illustrate this.

To convert this performance report into a form for recording the budget for this responsibility center, the minimum that is needed is shown in Figure 12.

The format in Figure 12, while apparently adequate, has several shortcomings. Before analyzing them, two points should be covered.

GMC: PERFORMANCE REPORT FOR FOREMAN – MACHINE SHOP

WEEK: _____ MONTH: _____ YEAR: _____

| YEAR TO DATE | | FINANCIAL PERFORMANCE ($) | | CURRENT PERIOD TOTAL | | LATHE SECTION | | MILLING SECTION | | OTHER MACHINES | |
ACTUAL	VARIANCE			ACTUAL	VARIANCE	ACTUAL	VARIANCE	ACTUAL	VARIANCE	ACTUAL	VARIANCE
		LABOR COMPENSATION	DIRECT								
			INDIRECT								
			TOTAL								
		LABOR RELATED BENEFITS									
		DIRECT MATERIALS									
		SUPPLIES & SMALL TOOLS									
		UTILITIES									
		REPAIRS & MAINTENANCE									
		OTHER OPERATING EXPENSES									
		TOTAL EXPENSES									
		OPERATIONAL INDICATORS									
		HEADCOUNT	DIRECT								
			INDIRECT								
			TOTAL								
		CAPACITY UTILIZATION (%)									
		ABSENTEEISM (%)									
		OVERTIME	$								
			HOURS								
		DOWNTIME (HOURS)	BREAKDOWNS								
			LACK OF OPERATOR								
			LACK OF R.M.								
			TOTAL								
		ACCIDENTS	#								
			SEVERITY								
		GRIEVANCES INITIATED									
		WORK-IN-PROCESS INVENTORY									
		PRODUCTION VOLUME									
		WORK ORDERS DELAYED									

Copy to: Manufacturing Manager

Figure 11. Performance report for a GMC responsibility center

SIMPLEST FORM OF BUDGET FOR THE GMC MACHINE SHOP

FINANCIAL PERFORMANCE ($)		TOTAL SHOP		LATHE SECTION		MILLING SECTION		OTHER MACHINES	
		ANNUAL BUDGET	AVERAGE WEEKLY BUDGET	ANNUAL BUDGET	AVERAGE WEEKLY BUDGET	ANNUAL BUDGET	AVERAGE WEEKLY BUDGET	ANNUAL BUDGET	AVERAGE WEEKLY BUDGET
LABOR COMPENSATION	DIRECT								
	INDIRECT								
	TOTAL								
LABOR RELATED BENEFITS									
DIRECT MATERIALS									
SUPPLIES & SMALL TOOLS									
UTILITIES		/////		/////		/////		/////	
REPAIRS & MAINTENANCE									
OTHER OPERATING EXPENSES									
TOTAL EXPENSES									
OPERATIONAL PERFORMANCE		/////		/////		/////		/////	
HEADCOUNT	DIRECT								
	INDIRECT								
	TOTAL								
CAPACITY UTILIZATION									
NORMAL ABSENTEEISM									
OVERTIME	$								
	HOURS								
WORK-IN-PROCESS INVENTORY									
PRODUCTION VOLUME									

Figure 12. Data sheet for recording budget information for a GMC responsibility center

First, the format assumes that the appropriate budget period is one year. This may or may not be suitable to your particular firm. Most budget experts agree that one year is the *minimum* time horizon you should consider. In many situations, a longer time period should be used. The selection of an appropriate time period for your firm will be discussed in detail in Section IX in the context of the profit budget.

Second, operational indicators—such as the number and severity of accidents and work-orders delayed—are not considered in the budget format. The presumption is that there will be no accidents or delays. That is, the budget for these kinds of indicators is zero.

Other indicators, such as machine downtime due to breakdowns, may sometimes be budgeted at a level above zero. This is a matter of choice you should make according to the needs of your firm. If it is unreasonable to expect that breakdowns can be avoided, despite adhering strictly to specified preventive maintenance practices, then you should specify a standard expectation for breakdown hours.

ANALYZING TYPICAL BUDGET FORM PROBLEMS

Many companies already possess budget forms they consider adequate. By pointing out some of the shortcomings in Figure 12, we hope to give you the basis for analyzing your own current forms for potential problem areas.

Some of the problems with Figure 12—which may plague your forms also—are:

1. The format does not give any indications of how reasonable the budget is in relation to past performance levels.
2. External factors that significantly affect the performance of the responsibility center are not identified.
3. There is no formal recognition of any changes in the level or kind of resources that will be made available to the responsibility center.
4. Assuming that performance is affected by seasonal factors, the average weekly performance recorded in the format may be meaningless.
5. There is no provision for stating the plans of the foreman to do things differently or better.

6. There is no mechanism to recognize and assess the impact on financial and operational performance of changes in the level of activity of the machine shop.

7. Fundamentally, the format serves as nothing more than a convenient way to record budget figures. It does not encourage or require that the managers developing these figures consider and analyze the various factors that are relevant to the development of truly meaningful budget figures.

DESIGNING A BETTER BUDGET FORM

You can design budgeting forms that force managers to recognize and analyze the factors that will affect the future performance of their responsibility centers by means of a six-step procedure.

First, you want to take into account past performance. This can be achieved in the machine shop form in Figure 12 by adding columns that report the shop's performance in the past two or three years. A column added with the percentage change over the past year's would force the foreman to recognize that trend.

All this information may require added pages. Thus, the past trend and budget for the total machine shop would be on the first page, and details for the lathe, milling and other sections on subsequent pages.

The second step is to include external factors in the form. These external factors could include the past and projected availability of skilled machinists. The product manager-residential products, for example, could keep track of housing starts as a valuable indicator of probable sales levels.

In addition to factors external to the firm as a whole, each responsibility center must recognize its obligations and commitments to the other responsibility centers in the firm. For instance, the machine shop's production volume is dictated by the projected deliveries of various kinds of meters, derived from GMC's sales budgets. In turn, the foundry's production will be determined by the machine shop's planned schedule for the budget period.

The budget format design should highlight such commitments to the other responsibility centers. The machine shop can accomplish this by emphasizing the critical importance of the "Production Volume" estimates and by supporting these estimates with more details about the type of jobs that are likely to be carried out.

FURTHER STEPS TOWARD THE BEST BUDGET FORM

The third step is to identify the levels of availability of key resources. This would recognize the impact of *internal* top management decisions.

For instance, capital expenditure plans may call for adding to the capacity of the machine shop by replacing some old milling machines with a new numerically controlled machine capable of a much greater production volume. Again, you should include the resource levels in past years so that the impact these resources have had on performance can be better understood.

The fourth step is to recognize the influence of seasonality. This is not important in all industries. But if there is marked and predictable variation in demand at various times in the year, then any form similar to Figure 12 is entirely inadequate. Soft drink companies, garment manufacturers, and building contractors operating in countries where climatic conditions vary greatly with the seasons must recognize seasonality.

Seasonality is an important consideration for GMC too, with its demand for residential products being a function of housing starts. GMC may find it adequate to break up the yearly volume figures into quarterly details. For other firms, monthly variations may be significant and predictable enough to require explicit recognition.

The fifth step is to formally record the major new actions that the head of the responsibility center plans to take. In fact, these plans of action are the foundation of budgets. Thus, the numbers recorded in the budget format should essentially reflect the consequence of taking the actions that are planned.

For example, clearly the foreman of the machine shop must have plans for installing the new numerically controlled milling machine. Job training for machinists may be another key program during the forthcoming budget period. These programs or plans of action must be recorded and included as part of the budget, with the following details:

1. Description of the action/program.
2. Person responsible for carrying out the action/program.
3. Person responsible for monitoring the effectiveness with which the action/program is executed.

4. Deadlines by which the action/program is to be completed and the scheduled time of completion of major components of the program.

5. Expected impact on performance, both financial and operational, of the action/program that is planned.

Section IX provides a complete program for these details based on a GMC example.

The sixth step is needed only in responsibility centers that are engineered expense centers (Type I). The machine shop in GMC is such. It is desirable to develop flexible budgets for costs that are not readily covered by standards. Material consumption and direct labor costs would be based on standards developed in Section IV.

However, overhead costs may require the development of flexible budgets. Essentially, there are budgets for the permissible level of overhead costs at various levels of activity.

AN EXAMPLE OF A COMPREHENSIVE BUDGETING FORM

Employing the six step procedure detailed above would result in a much more detailed budget format than the one illustrated in Figure 12. A better budget format for the machine shop is given in Figures 13, 14 and 15.

Note: The desirability of having a format that does not exceed one page does not apply to *budgeting* formats, only to *reporting* formats. We have always found it better to have more detail when designing budget formats. The desirability and usefulness of having action plans and performance expectations described in detail are particularly evident when you have to review actual performance in relation to budgeted performance.

The circled numbers in each Figure focus on how the format responds to the six steps discussed above, namely:

1. Consider past performance trends.
2. Analyze external factors.
3. Identify the level of resource availability.
4. Recognize the impact of seasonality.
5. Articulate the underlying action plans/programs.
6. Develop flexible budgets for overhead costs, if appropriate.

RECOMMENDED BUDGET FORMAT FOR THE GMC MACHINE SHOP

ACTUAL 198X-3 ①	ACTUAL 198X-2 ①	ACTUAL 198X-1 ①	TOTAL BUDGET FOR 198X	% CHANGE (COMPOUNDED) 198X-3 to 198X-1 ①	CHANGE 198X-1 to 198X ①	FINANCIAL PERFORMANCE	FIRST QUARTER		SECOND QUARTER		THIRD QUARTER		FOURTH QUARTER	
							TOTAL ④	AVERAGE WEEKLY BUDGET ④	TOTAL ④	AVERAGE WEEKLY BUDGET ④	TOTAL ④	AVERAGE WEEKLY BUDGET ④	TOTAL ④	AVERAGE WEEKLY BUDGET ④
						LABOR COMPENSATION — DIRECT								
						LABOR COMPENSATION — INDIRECT								
						LABOR COMPENSATION — TOTAL								
						LABOR RELATED BENEFITS								
						DIRECT MATERIALS								
						SUPPLIES & SMALL TOOLS								
						UTILITIES								
						REPAIRS & MAINTENANCE								
						OTHER OPERATING EXPENSES								
						TOTAL EXPENSES								
						EXTERNAL FACTORS/ RESOURCES								
						ESTIMATED AVAILABILITY OF MACHINISTS (APPLICATIONS?) ②								
						VALUE OF P & E ③								
						OPERATIONAL PERFORMANCE								
						PRODUCTION VOLUME (BASED ON SALES BUDGET) ②								
						HEAD COUNT — DIRECT								
						HEAD COUNT — INDIRECT								
						HEAD COUNT — TOTAL								
						CAPACITY UTILIZATION (%)								
						NORMAL ABSENTEEISM (%)								
						OVERTIME — $								
						OVERTIME — HOURS								
						WORK-IN-PROCESS INVENTORY								

Figure 13. A comprehensive budget format for the GMC machine shop

SECTION-WISE BUDGET	L A T H E S E C T I O N								
		FIRST QUARTER		SECOND QUARTER		THIRD QUARTER		FOURTH QUARTER	
FINANCIAL PERFORMANCE	ANNUAL TOTAL	TOTAL ④	AVERAGE WEEKLY BUDGET ④	TOTAL ④	AVERAGE WEEKLY BUDGET ④	TOTAL ④	AVERAGE WEEKLY BUDGET ④	TOTAL ④	AVERAGE WEEKLY BUDGET ④
LABOR COMPENSATION — DIRECT									
LABOR COMPENSATION — INDIRECT									
LABOR COMPENSATION — TOTAL									
LABOR-RELATED BENEFITS									
DIRECT MATERIALS									
SUPPLIES & SMALL TOOLS									
UTILITIES									
REPAIRS & MAINTENANCE									
OTHER OPERATING EXPENSES									
TOTAL EXPENSES									
EXTERNAL FACTORS/RESOURCES									
ADDITIONAL MACHINISTS ②									
VALUE OF EQUIPMENT ③									
OPERATIONAL PERFORMANCE									
PRODUCTION VOLUME ②									
HEAD COUNT — DIRECT									
HEAD COUNT — INDIRECT									
HEAD COUNT — TOTAL									
CAPACITY UTILIZATION (%)									
NORMAL ABSENTEEISM (%)									
OVERTIME $									
OVERTIME HOURS									
WORK-IN-PROCESS INVENTORY									

Figure 14. The GMC machine shop budget format by section

SECTION-WISE BUDGET

MILLING SECTION

FINANCIAL PERFORMANCE		ANNUAL TOTAL	FIRST QUARTER		SECOND QUARTER		THIRD QUARTER		FOURTH QUARTER	
			TOTAL ④	AVERAGE WEEKLY BUDGET ④	TOTAL ④	AVERAGE WEEKLY BUDGET ④	TOTAL ④	AVERAGE WEEKLY BUDGET ④	TOTAL ④	AVERAGE WEEKLY BUDGET ④
LABOR COMPENSATION	DIRECT									
	INDIRECT									
	TOTAL									
LABOR-RELATED BENEFITS										
DIRECT MATERIALS										
SUPPLIES & SMALL TOOLS										
UTILITIES										
REPAIRS & MAINTENANCE										
OTHER OPERATING EXPENSES										
TOTAL EXPENSES										
EXTERNAL FACTORS/ RESOURCES										
ADDITIONAL MACHINISTS ②										
VALUE OF EQUIPMENT ③										
OPERATIONAL PERFORMANCE										
PRODUCTION VOLUME ②										
HEAD COUNT	DIRECT									
	INDIRECT									
	TOTAL									
CAPACITY UTILIZATION (%)										
NORMAL ABSENTEEISM (%)										
OVERTIME	$									
	HOURS									
WORK-IN-PROCESS INVENTORY										

Figure 14. Continued

SECTION-WISE BUDGET

OTHER SECTIONS

FINANCIAL PERFORMANCE		ANNUAL TOTAL	FIRST QUARTER		SECOND QUARTER		THIRD QUARTER		FOURTH QUARTER	
			TOTAL ④	AVERAGE WEEKLY BUDGET ④	TOTAL ④	AVERAGE WEEKLY BUDGET ④	TOTAL ④	AVERAGE WEEKLY BUDGET ④	TOTAL ④	AVERAGE WEEKLY BUDGET ④
LABOR COMPENSATION	DIRECT									
	INDIRECT									
	TOTAL									
LABOR-RELATED BENEFITS										
DIRECT MATERIALS										
SUPPLIES & SMALL TOOLS										
UTILITIES										
REPAIRS & MAINTENANCE										
OTHER OPERATING EXPENSES										
TOTAL EXPENSES										
EXTERNAL FACTORS/RESOURCES		/////	/////	/////	/////	/////	/////	/////	/////	/////
ADDITIONAL MACHINISTS ②				/////		/////		/////		/////
VALUE OF EQUIPMENT ③		/////		/////		/////		/////		/////
OPERATIONAL PERFORMANCE		/////	/////	/////	/////	/////	/////	/////	/////	/////
PRODUCTION VOLUME ②										
HEAD COUNT	DIRECT									
	INDIRECT									
	TOTAL									
CAPACITY UTILIZATION (%)										
NORMAL ABSENTEEISM (%)										
OVERTIME	$									
	HOURS									
WORK-IN-PROCESS INVENTORY										

Figure 14. Continued

FLEXIBLE OVERHEAD BUDGET ⑥

BUDGET ITEM		85% OF NORMAL CAPACITY (PRODUCTION VOLUME: ----)				90% OF NORMAL CAPACITY (PRODUCTION VOLUME: ----)				95% OF NORMAL CAPACITY (PRODUCTION VOLUME: ----)				100% OF NORMAL CAPACITY (PRODUCTION VOLUME: ----)				105% OF NORMAL CAPACITY (PRODUCTION VOLUME: ----)			
		TOTAL	LATHE	MILLING	OTHER	TOTAL	LATHE	MILLING	OTHER	TOTAL	LATHE	MILLING	OTHER	TOTAL	LATHE	MILLING	OTHER	TOTAL	LATHE	MILLING	OTHER
INDIRECT LABOR	WAGES																				
	BENEFITS																				
	TOTAL																				
SUPPLIES & SMALL TOOLS																					
UTILITIES																					
REPAIRS & MAINTENANCE																					
OTHER OPERATING EXPENSES																					
TOTAL EXPENSES																					

Figure 15. Additional forms for flexible budget analysis

SERIAL NO.	ACTION/PROGRAM DESCRIPTION	EXECUTIVE RESPONSIBILITY	MONITORING RESPONSIBILITY	COMPLETION DEADLINE AND SELECTED MILESTONES	IMPACT ON PERFORMANCE	
					PRIOR TO ACTION/PROGRAM	AFTER COMPLETION

ACTION PLAN DOCUMENTATION ⑤

Figure 15. Continued

COST ACCOUNTING SYSTEMS AND THE PRODUCTION BUDGET

The cost accounting system in most firms is the source of most accounting information contained in the firms' production budgets and reports. Cost accounting systems should serve at least three major purposes:

1. Valuation of production and inventories, particularly work-in-process and finished goods inventories, providing the cost of goods sold figures for the income statement and inventory values for the balance sheet.

2. Control of direct costs and overheads, particularly manufacturing costs.

3. Planning of revenue-related decisions such as pricing and product mix.

From the managerial standpoint, the last two purposes are much more important than the first. Unfortunately, the valuation of inventories was the initial purpose of cost accounting systems and still continues to be the primary consideration determining their design. This is unfortunate because most systems, as a result, tend to be very poorly suited to the needs of budgeting and managerial control.

Some of the major flaws common to design of cost accounting systems are described below. You should analyze your own system to ensure it doesn't include these shortcomings.

ACCOUNTING FOR DIRECT MATERIAL

The system for accounting for direct material is relatively easy since it involves tangible items. Depending on whether a job costing or process costing system is appropriate to your firm, you can easily track the issue of new materials to specific work orders or departments, respectively, through the mandatory use of requisition slips with the necessary details.

The cost accounting system should identify at least two reasons for variances from budgeted or standard consumption of materials. One variance would be due to a difference in the price paid from the standard or budgeted price, i.e., the *"price variance."*

A second difference would be in the quantity of material consumed compared to the budgeted or standard quantity, i.e., the *"quantity or usage variance."* The price variance is often wrongly generated or wrongly interpreted and used. The usage variance is less difficult to identify and interpret.

GENERATING PRICE VARIANCES

The first common error relating to the price variance is the point in time at which it is generated. Assume that in GMC the manufacturing manager's office carries out the purchasing function. Figure 16 illustrates two systems for generating the price variance and identifies the better method.

The first method produces information on a timely basis regarding the changes in material prices from the standard prices. The second method is inferior because the price variance is generated at the time the material is issued to the production shop.

Moreover, the price variance is generated piecemeal since the quantities issued at any one time may be much smaller than the total quantity purchased at one particular time. The second method is sometimes considered adequate, and indeed preferable, from the point of view of *allocating* actual material costs to the products that are manufactured.

We cannot overemphasize the importance of generating price variances at the time the material is purchased. On occasion, the time period between purchase and issue of the material may be so long that the variances generated by the second method are meaningless.

Price variances should trigger managerial action. Perhaps purchase requisitions are not being generated early enough to give the purchase officer enough time to pick the sources offering the lowest price. Or the efficiency of the purchase section may need to be improved. Or the price at which the products that use these raw materials are sold may need to be changed. Or perhaps management should even seek alternative sources, substitute materials, different product designs or different products.

ANOTHER PROBLEM WITH PRICE VARIANCES

The second common misconception about price variances is that they are not worth the effort involved in generating them. Two reasons are frequently given. One is that there are too many different materials and

METHOD I: (RECOMMENDED)

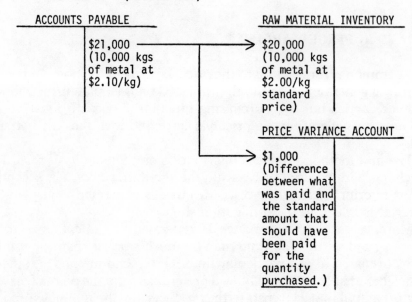

ACCOUNTS PAYABLE

$21,000
(10,000 kgs
of metal at
$2.10/kg)

RAW MATERIAL INVENTORY

$20,000
(10,000 kgs
of metal at
$2.00/kg
standard
price)

PRICE VARIANCE ACCOUNT

$1,000
(Difference
between what
was paid and
the standard
amount that
should have
been paid
for the
quantity
purchased.)

METHOD 2:   (NOT RECOMMENDED)

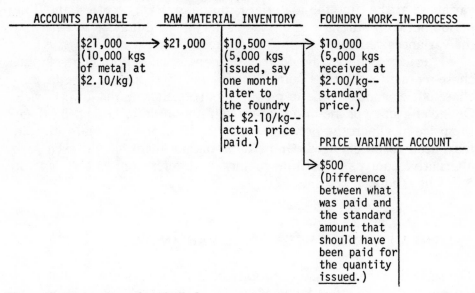

ACCOUNTS PAYABLE   RAW MATERIAL INVENTORY   FOUNDRY WORK-IN-PROCESS

$21,000 ──→ $21,000 $10,500 ── $10,000
(10,000 kgs   (5,000 kgs   (5,000 kgs
of metal at   issued, say   received at
$2.10/kg)   one month $2.00/kg--
                      later to   standard
                      the foundry   price.)
                      at $2.10/kg--
                      actual price   PRICE VARIANCE ACCOUNT
                      paid.)
                                           $500
                                           (Difference
                                           between what
                                           was paid and
                                           the standard
                                           amount that
                                           should have
                                           been paid for
                                           the quantity
                                           issued.)

Figure 16. Comparison of methods for generating price variances

components to be purchased, and that developing price expectations and calculating price variances is too demanding a task. The other is that the purchase managers cannot generally be held responsible for price variances because the causes of these variances are uncontrollable. Both these reasons are unacceptable.

It is both unnecessary and undesirable to develop price standards and price variances for *all* the different materials purchased by your firm. The technique of "ABC Analysis" responds to the problem of too many different items.

You should develop standards and variances only for the "A" items that are purchased. These "A" items are the 20% of total items that in most firms account for 80% of the money spent on materials. You can safely exclude the "B" and "C" items in inventory, which constitute by far the largest number, and treat their actual prices as standard.

The argument that purchase managers cannot normally be held responsible for price variances is irrelevant. Price variances are not needed to find fault with the purchase manager. They are needed to trigger remedial actions, such as changing sales prices, vendors, materials, product designs, etc. Unless you set a standard materials price on which decisions regarding sales prices, product mix and so forth can be based, there is no meaningful way your organization can plan or budget its profits or identify situations where these decisions need to be modified.

Moreover, the exercise of setting price standards for the "A" items forces the purchasing executives to evaluate and plan sources, timing and quantity of purchases. Price standards are also necessary so that you can appropriately identify the responsibility of the production departments. Barring exceptional circumstances, the production departments cannot be held responsible for the impact of price variances on the cost of producing goods.

By extracting price variances and charging the standard price for materials issued to the production departments, only quantity variances are included in their reports. The separation of price and quantity variances greatly facilitates performance review and the identification of appropriate remedial action.

ADDRESSING USAGE VARIANCES

Tracking and recording usage variances is a much simpler task. In fact, an effective method is to issue only predetermined standard quantities of raw materials for each work order. Additional requests for material for a work order already serviced would be charged to the materials usage variance account for the concerned responsibility center.

Also, if the output of the responsibility center does not conform to the quantity specified in the work order, the standard quantity of materials needed to produce the difference would again be charged to it.

Cost accounting textbooks of a scholarly nature often spend an inordinate amount of time discussing the interrelated character of material price and usage variances. They stress the fact that different methods would give rise to different figures for these two components of the total materials variances. In our opinion, this controversy is of little or no significance from the practicing manager's point of view. The method of calculating price variances at the time of issue is clearly the best from the point of view of triggering managerial action. Further refinements are unnecessary and possibly inappropriate.

ACCOUNTING FOR DIRECT LABOR

Labor costs that can be directly traced to the products being manufactured should in general be analyzed in terms of two variances. First, there is the labor "efficiency variance," which is analogous to the material "usage variance." Second, there is the labor "rate variance," which is analogous to the material "price variance."

Generating these labor variances creates no unusual problems. Time cards filled in by each worker or his superior identify the job numbers or work orders on which time is spent. The accounting office adds data regarding standard time for the work carried out, standard wage rates for the responsibility center and actual wages paid to the worker. The rate and efficiency variances for the responsibility center can readily be calculated from these data.

ACCOUNTING FOR OVERHEAD

Overheads, i.e., costs that cannot be directly traced to products (or which are individually not significant enough to warrant a system that could directly attach them to the products), have been consistently growing as a proportion of total costs in most industries. The problem is that the traditional overhead budgeting techniques are oriented more toward allocating overhead costs to the products, rather than providing ways to better plan and control these increasingly significant costs.

Several studies and our experience have shown that most overhead budgeting systems are unnecessarily complex. This results in a variety of variances that are usually not understood by managers receiving reports on them. There are two major concerns regarding the budgeting of overhead costs.

First, in order to control overhead costs, it is necessary that your cost accounting system distinguish between overhead costs that are *relatable* to the responsibility center and those that are *allocated* to the responsibility center.

For example, in the GMC machine shop, supplies and small tools are relatable overhead. The cost of the supplies and small tools consumed by the machine shop is directly identifiable from the stores' records. But these supplies and small tool costs are *overhead* costs rather than *direct material* costs because the proportion consumed by each job order, work order, product line or product cannot be physically tracked. It must be allocated to the products on some rational basis.

While these are clearly overhead costs, they are very different from other overhead terms, such as the proportion of the manufacturing manager's salary that may be *allocated* to the machine shop by the cost accountant in order to attach a reasonable proportion of it to each product or product line.

Relatable overheads are usually subject to the control of the manager of the responsibility center. Allocated overheads are not. Your accounting system should distinguish between these two types of overhead costs. In fact, our experience has often found it desirable to exclude allocated overheads in performance reports intended for control purposes.

ANOTHER CONCERN OF OVERHEAD BUDGETING

The second major set of concerns relating to the overhead budget is that too many variances are generated. In one large firm, the accounting system generated five overhead variances, labeled "volume," "seasonal," "calendar," "spending," and "efficiency."

These fine distinctions were confusing rather than helpful or informative.

The performance reports we recommend ignore the "volume," "seasonal," and "calendar" variances. All the information that they provided was more simply and directly provided by the variance from budgeted production volume.

The distinction between "spending" and "efficiency" variances is certainly meaningful. But they can be combined into a single "controllable" variance derived by comparing actual overhead costs to the costs budgeted for the actual level of production.

The "step chart" approach to flexible budgets for overheads is simpler to understand and more informative than the more complex aggregated methods. Under the latter method, volume, spending, and efficiency variances are generated from budget equations that assume costs are either fixed or variable, and all fixed costs and all variable costs are aggregated.

The variances generated by the use of budget equations do not identify which items of overhead were responsible, and are more theoretical than realistic.

An example of a "step chart" for the flexible overhead budget is shown in Figure 15. The variances between the actual costs incurred for each listed item and the standard figures at the appropriate capacity level drawn from the step chart, combined with the production volume variance, give you all the information that the more complex systems provide. Moreover, these variances can readily be understood, can be related to actual happenings, and can swiftly point to needed remedial action.

ACTION REQUIREMENTS

Identify the responsibility centers that are engineered expense centers (Type I). Most, if not all, of your production-manufacturing responsibility centers will fall into this category. Using the performance reports designed in Section III, develop budgeting formats that will force the managers of the responsibility centers to take into account the factors that influence and help plan performance. These include:

1. Past performance
2. External factors

3. Resource availability

4. Seasonality trends

5. Action plans/programs

6. Flexible budgets

The step-by-step approach described in this Section should enable you to develop effective budget formats with a minimum of difficulty.

It is also useful to review your cost accounting system at this stage. In particular, examine the method of generating price variances for materials. The system should generate material "price" and "quantity-usage" variances and labor "rate" and "efficiency" variances.

If your firm already has flexible overhead budgets, these can be easily translated into the step charts that are part of the budget format design. You must ensure that you make the distinction between "relatable" and "allocated" overhead.

Finally, the material, labor and overhead standards that have been developed (described in Section IV) can be entered into the budgeting formats or attached as supporting data for subsequent calculation of expected performance figures. The process within the firm by which the budgeting forms will be filled in with appropriate figures is discussed in detail in Section X.

VI

Preparing the Sales Budget

In most firms, the sales budget is the basis of other budgets, such as the production budget. Firms where production constraints influence sales and other budgets are an exception. However, even in countries where governmental regulations and licensing practices control capacity expansion, continued shortages of production capacity normally trigger investments to increase this capacity. Developing the sales budget is therefore particularly important.

The sales budget is more difficult to develop than the production budget. The uncertainties are greater and the alternatives are more numerous.

The production budget applies primarily to engineered expense centers (Type I units where the process and outputs are known and measurable). Technological considerations often limit the available alternatives.

Sales budgets apply to revenue and contribution centers. Both are Type II units where the process is not well-defined, though the outputs are measurable. The interaction with the external environment of the firm is explicit and extensive. The variables in revenue and contribution centers are more numerous and less well understood than the variables in engineered expense centers.

THE BASIS FOR THE SALES BUDGET

All these considerations reinforce some basic conclusions. Your firm must pay careful attention to developing the sales budget. You must encourage creativity and allow greater discretion to the managers of revenue and contribution centers than you do the managers of engineered expense centers.

A critical decision influencing the nature of the sales budget is whether you decide to treat the concerned responsibility center as a revenue center or a contribution center. Section II discussed that issue using the examples of the product manager-residential products and the product manager-industrial products at GMC.

The key criterion to determine the nature of the sales responsibility center should be whether the manager of the responsibility center should have control over the selling price of the products he deals with.

In the case of the product manager-residential products, the marketing manager decided on the price at which the residential products were to be sold. Consequently, the residential products responsibility center was defined as a revenue center.

Because a revenue center is simpler to budget for than a contribution center, the characteristics of budgets in revenue centers will be discussed before taking up the design of budgets for contribution centers.

BUDGETS FOR REVENUE CENTERS

The responsibility of the product manager-residential products is to generate maximum unit sales within the constraints of the output of the manufacturing function. Also, he has to operate with the selling prices determined by the marketing manager. The resources or inputs available to him are the six salespeople reporting to him. In addition, the inputs to this responsibility center include the residential meters produced by the manufacturing department.

The performance report for this revenue center (designed to

guidelines in Section III) is the starting point for developing the budget format. The step-by-step procedure would incorporate:

1. Past performance
2. External factors
3. Resource availability
4. Seasonality trends
5. Action plans-programs.

The flexible budgets suggested for overhead costs in production units are usually inappropriate for revenue centers. Pre-sale marketing costs do not necessarily vary with sales levels. Post-sale distribution costs can be controlled with the use of standards.

The best approach is to specify the inputs—personnel, products— that will be made available to the revenue center. Following the tentative determination of feasible resource levels, you can analyze the possibilities for revenue generation and fix a figure for revenues to be budgeted. A procedure that examines the relationship between sales potential and needed inputs to achieve this potential would be desirable.

The procedure here is identical to the step-by-step procedure demonstrated for the production budget. The importance of external factors is greater in the case of revenue centers than in production centers, and you may have to analyze external sales possibilities in a detailed fashion.

The product-market matrix diagrammed in Table 5 is very useful for directing the analysis of sales potential.

The matrix in Table 5 categorizes the possibilities for increasing revenue in a manner that encourages consideration of all possibilities. It also serves as a basis to develop the action plans-programs that express and structure the manager's plans for the budget period.

The personnel who should be involved in the process of identifying sales potential in each of the four categories are identified in the matrix—field salespeople for old products for old customers and territories, for example.

Action plans based on this matrix and the involvement of the appropriate personnel greatly facilitate the identification of causes if actual revenues differ from those budgeted. They would also aid in the speedy determination of remedial action.

In short, revenue centers require very simple *fixed* budgets for:

PRODUCTS

	OLD	NEW
OLD CUSTOMERS AND TERRITORIES	Based largely on historical data and inputs from field salespeople.	Based on inputs from R&D, manufacturing and field salespeople.
NEW CUSTOMERS AND TERRITORIES	Based on inputs from field salespeople.	Based on inputs from R&D, manufacturing and focussed market research.

MARKETS

Table 5. A product-market matrix diagram

1. revenues to be generated; and
2. expenses to be incurred.

Those budgets are based on the projected availability of products from the manufacturing department matched with the perceived potential for sales of both old and new products to old and new markets.

BUDGETS FOR CONTRIBUTION CENTERS

In contrast to the budgets for revenue centers, the budgets for contribution centers are relatively complex. In our hypothetical company, the product manager-industrial products has the authority to decide the price at which industrial meters are to be sold. So evaluating him on revenues generated would be inadequate and inappropriate.

In order to recognize the interrelationship of prices, costs and volumes, an artificial profit figure must be developed as a basis for evaluating sales units where the manager has control over the pricing decision. A drop in units sold might not mean that performance is bad. In fact, the increased price at which this reduced number of units is sold might have a positive impact on profits. The cost of manufacturing the products is a key consideration in determining price, as marginal pricing based on incremental costs may be a relevant consideration, particularly in competitive bidding situations.

This means that contribution centers, unlike revenue centers, must pay a price for the products provided to them. The *contribution* to overheads and profits made by the contribution center would then be determined as follows:

	Revenues generated	: $100
Less	Transfer price of products sold	: (45)
Less	Costs directly relatable to the center	: (25)
Equals	Contribution	: $ 30

The figure of contribution is the key effectiveness measure. Revenues generated are easy to measure. So also are costs that can be directly related and *not allocated* to the contribution center. The specification of the transfer price is therefore the critical decision to be made in calculating the contribution.

TRANSFER PRICING FOR CONTRIBUTION CENTERS

There are basically only two alternatives to determine the transfer price. The first is to specify the "full cost" of manufacturing the product as the transfer price. This cost would include the direct material, direct labor and an allocated proportion of manufacturing overheads. This is the most widely used approach, with variations that include a mark-up on the full costs. This "full cost" method is not the best because it leads to wrong decisions by the manager of the contribution center.

The second alternative is to specify that the transfer price should be the variable manufacturing costs relatable to the products. This method leads to the right profit-maximizing decisions by the manager of the contribution center. Figure 17 illustrates the superiority of this alternative.

COMPARISON OF TRANSFER PRICING ALTERNATIVES

Line No.	Manufacturing Department Assumptions	Alternative 1 ("Full Cost")	Alternative 2 ("Variable/ Marginal Cost")
1.	Variable cost per unit of product	$20.00	$20.00
2.	Fixed costs—total	$20,000.00	$20,000.00
3.	Budgeted production	2,000 units	2,000 units
4.	Fixed costs—per unit	$10.00	$10.00
5.	"Full cost"	$30.00	$30.00
6.	Transfer price	$30.00	$20.00
	Contribution Center Assumptions		
7.	Variable costs per unit— transfer price	$30.00	$20.00
8.	Variable costs per unit— relatable marketing costs	$10.00	$10.00
9.	Variable costs per unit—total	$40.00	$30.00
10.	Selling price per unit	$50.00	$50.00
11.	Contribution per unit	$10.00	$20.00
12.	*Decision:* if an increase in marketing costs of $100.00 is expected to increase unit sales by 6 units	Do not increase mktg. costs [($10 × 6) − $100 = Loss]	Increase mktg. costs [($20 × 6) − $100 = Profit]
13.	Correct decision (because contribution to firm's profits is [$50 − $30] × 6 units less $100 = 20)	Increase	Increase

Figure 17. Two alternative methods for transfer pricing

ANALYZING ALTERNATIVE METHODS

The different decisions that transfer pricing (based on full costs and on variable costs) can give rise to in the same firm are in the columns. The "full cost" method is illustrated in Alternative 1 and the "variable cost" or "marginal cost" method is in Alternative 2.

Line 1 gives the variable (marginal) cost of manufacturing one unit of product. The $20 variable cost is the same under both methods. This number is a constant assuming a reasonable and limited range of volume.

Line 2 gives the total fixed costs, again assuming a limited range of volumes. Line 3 indicates the volume which was planned. Line 4 is obtained by dividing the total fixed costs (Line 2, $20,000) by the budgeted production (Line 3, 2,000 units).

The "full cost" or "absorption cost" of a unit of the product is given in Line 5 ($30). You obtain it by adding the variable cost per unit (Line 1, $20) and the fixed cost per unit (Line 4, $10).

The transfer price (Line 6) is the crucial difference between the two methods. Under the "full cost" alternative, the transfer price is the full cost calculated on Line 5. Under the "variable cost" alternative, the transfer price is the variable cost indicated in Line 1.

Lines 7 through 13 reflect the point of view of the manager of the contribution center. To calculate the variable (incremental/marginal) cost to the contribution center of selling one more unit, the costs that the manager looks at are the transfer price (Line 7) paid to the manufacturing department or corporate headquarters for each unit of product, and the marketing costs (Line 8) incurred per unit by the contribution center.

Under the "full cost" alternative, this cost (Line 9) is $40, while under the variable cost approach, it is $30 because the transfer price is less. This difference under the two methods affects subsequent calculations.

For example, when calculating the contribution per unit (Line 11) by subtracting the variable cost (Line 9) from the selling price per unit ($50, Line 10), the figures vary depending on the method chosen.

Consequently, managerial decisions will be different as indicated in Line 12, despite the fact that the actual economics of the situation are the same under both systems. The different decisions result from changes in the accounting system, not because the costs and revenues are different.

WEIGHING THE DECISION

The hypothetical decision (Line 12) is whether or not to incur an additional marketing expense of $100, if resultant sales increase by six units. Under the "full cost" alternative, the manager of the contribution center calculates that the increased contribution ($60) resulting from the additional sales will not cover the expense of $100. The calculations indicate a decrease in reported contribution of $40 if the expense is incurred and six additional units are sold.

Under the variable cost alternative, the increase in contribution resulting from an increase in sales of six units ($120) more than covers the additional expense of $100. The reported contribution would increase by $20 if the expense is incurred and six additional units are sold.

Clearly, both methods of transfer pricing cannot be right because each leads to a different decision. The manager of the responsibility center makes the correct decision when transfer prices are based on variable or marginal manufacturing costs.

The correct decision occurs when variable costs are the basis of transfer prices because the contribution figure on which the manager of the responsibility center bases his decisions is the correct contribution figure from the perspective of the firm. "Contribution" in economics is the difference between selling price and variable costs. The contribution figure is the same from the points of view of the general manager of GMC and the product manager-industrial products, if variable costs are the basis of the transfer price in GMC.

ADDRESSING PERCEIVED DRAWBACKS TO TRANSFER PRICING

Managers often express several reservations about the recommended method of transfer pricing. First, there is the argument that the apparent profitability of such contribution centers will be very high since manufacturing fixed costs are ignored. This could lead to misunderstandings about the relative importance of the manager of the contribution center.

One way to respond to this psychological—not economic—problem is to deduct a *fixed amount* approximately equal to manufacturing fixed costs before reporting the center's contribution figure. Care must be taken to *avoid* deducting *a fixed cost per unit*. This would convert the transfer-pricing system into the undesirable "full-cost" method.

The second major concern is whether the manufacturing department should also be converted into a profit center by crediting it with revenues equal to the transfer price debited to the contribution center. This would assuage the feeling on the part of production executives that they are otherwise seen as generating only expenses, not profits. It is easier and more appropriate to manage them as engineered expense centers, however.

The third concern is the accounting problem created by this artificial cost charged to contribution centers, if the manufacturing departments don't receive a balancing credit. The technical response is very simple. The marketing manager's report or the general manager's report (preferably the latter) could have a counterbalancing entry that would eliminate the problem.

The fourth issue often raised is about the accounting and economic justification of the transfer-pricing practice. The control system attempts to ensure that subordinate managers take the decisions and actions that superior managers would wish them to take. The transfer-pricing system based on variable manufacturing costs ensures that the managers of contribution centers make the right decisions from the point of view of the firm as a whole.

THE RELATIVE CONTRIBUTION APPROACH

The discussion of the multiple dimensions of information in Section II has particular relevance to the design of budgeting formats for contribution centers. These multiple dimensions are important in directing the analysis of alternatives in a creative and comprehensive fashion.

Sales are generated by products, in territories, and from customers. You can analyze any or all of these sources of revenue in the case of contribution centers to determine the most profitable products, territories and customers. The "relative contribution" generated by categories within each of these dimensions is a valuable input to develop the optimal contribution budget.

That relative contribution figure is calculated by deducting from the contribution generated by each product line, territorial location or customer type those fixed costs that would no longer be incurred if the revenues were sacrificed. Figure 18 is an example based on territories.

It indicates an apparently profitable marketing department. The department contributes $270,000 to manufacturing fixed costs, corporate overheads and profits. That $270,000 contribution figure may or may not result in profits for the firm. That depends on the magnitude of manufacturing fixed costs and other corporate overheads.

However, it is important to recognize that looking at the territorial (regional) dimension of information reveals that eliminating Region 2 could increase this contribution figure to $280,000. Without calculating the relative contribution of each region, this possible avenue for improving profits may not have been identified by the marketing department.

Similarly, it should prove worthwhile to calculate the relative contribution of other dimensions, such as customer types and product lines.

The design of budget formats for contribution centers is not the primary concern of the systems designer. The simple step-by-step procedure discussed for revenue centers is applicable here also. The major issue to resolve for contribution centers is the transfer-pricing system for products received from manufacturing.

Also, as in the case of revenue centers, the quality of analysis that goes into generating and evaluating creative alternatives for improving profitability is crucial. The relative contribution approach is valuable in this regard.

ACTION REQUIREMENTS

Identify the responsibility centers which sell your firm's products. Determine whether they are revenue centers (Type II) or contribution centers (also Type II), based on whether their managers make or substantially influence the pricing decision. This determination emerges from the designing of the performance reports as recommended in Section III.

Start with these performance reports. Proceed step-by-step to develop budget formats to force managers to consider past performance, external factors, resource availability, seasonality trends, and action plans or programs.

THE RELATIVE CONTRIBUTION APPROACH

	Total	Region 1	Region 2	Region 3	Region 4
Sales revenue	$6,850,000	$1,750,000	$600,000	$2,000,000	$2,500,000
Variable costs (including transfer prices)	5,480,000	1,400,000	480,000	1,600,000	2,000,000
Contribution before relatable costs	$1,370,000	$ 350,000	$120,000	$ 400,000	$ 500,000
Relatable regional costs (avoidable if region is dropped)	800,000	200,000	130,000	220,000	250,000
Relative regional contribution		$ 150,000	($10,000)	$ 180,000	$ 250,000
Remaining marketing costs	300,000				
Relative marketing contribution	$ 270,000				

If region 2 is dropped, impact on marketing contribution:

1. Reduction in revenues   = ($600,000)
2. Reduction in variable costs   = $480,000
3. Elimination of avoidable costs   = $130,000
4. Net impact   = $ 10,000 (+ ve)

Figure 18. Calculation of relative contribution by territory

Next, make sure you have the cost accounting information available to identify variable manufacturing costs to determine the transfer prices for your contribution centers.

You may find it desirable to review these manufacturing costs with the managers from the concerned manufacturing units and contribution centers. Impartial, knowledgeable personnel from the accounting and industrial engineering departments should also be present to clarify areas of doubt or misunderstanding regarding manufacturing costs.

Finally, familiarize the revenue center and contribution center managers with the product-market matrix and the relative contribution approach as techniques for structuring the generation and evaluation of alternatives for improving revenues and profits.

VII

Analyzing
Staff Function Budgets

Most staff departments fall into the category of discretionary expense centers, where the relationship between the inputs (dollars) and the outputs (physical) is a matter of judgment. They can be either Type II or Type III units where the process or outputs are not well defined. Usually they are Type III units. In developing budgets for staff departments, it is important to understand the character of each department so that you can select the appropriate planning and control techniques.

TYPICAL STAFF DEPARTMENTS

Purchasing departments lend themselves to a variety of such techniques. Standards can be applied for routine activities, such as the processing of purchase requisitions, overbuying and over-delivery, and percentage increases vs. general index. Effectiveness measures are very important for purchasing departments.

For instance, raw material stockouts due to delays by the purchasing department are an important measure of how effectively the department is functioning. When most purchases are routine in nature, this department takes on the character of an engineered expense center and efficiency measures become meaningful.

The number of purchase requisitions handled and the dollar amount of purchases made serve as measures of the output. The cost and number of personnel in the purchasing department are the input measures, when calculating efficiency.

The purchase price variance discussed in Section IV regarding production budgets is of great value to the purchasing department as a basis of *planning* improved purchasing practices. The price variances as a *control* device to evelute the purchasing department must be employed with caution because of possible uncontrollable factors affecting price.

To summarize, in purchasing departments:

1. Develop *standards* for routine, repetitive activities.
2. Focus on *effectiveness* (stockouts, quality and price variances).
3. Add *efficiency* measures if large numbers of routine purchases are made.

Maintenance departments, for planning and control, are similar to purchasing departments. You should develop standards for repetitive jobs, either preventive or breakdown. Subjective or theoretical standards for major jobs that involve substantial production volume may be useful, even though the frequency of occurrence or repetition is low.

Effectiveness measures such as downtime due to poor maintenance or delays in maintenance are also important. Efficiency measures are, however, more easily developed and applied to maintenance departments. This is because effectiveness measures would require difficult subjective assessments of the quality of the work done by the maintenance department.

Such assessments of quality are often a source of discord and conflict. Efficiency measures would, in contrast, focus on the time and cost of completing specific jobs and require less subjective assessments of quality.

To summarize, in maintenance departments:

1. Develop *standards* for repetitive maintenance activities, both preventive and breakdown.
2. Focus on *efficiency* measures (time and cost to complete jobs).

3. Add *effectiveness* measures (downtime due to poor or delayed maintenance) when reasonably objective assessments of the quality of the maintenance work can be made.

OTHER TYPICAL STAFF DEPARTMENTS

Computer services and *accounting* departments are more difficult to manage than the previous two types of staff departments. Standards and process-oriented controls are often inappropriate for these types of staff departments. Often, it is best to limit their measurements to the timeliness or accuracy of the promised services.

When repetitive, routine activities are significant in these departments, standards become desirable. Such standards could be set, for instance, for the number of data entry keystrokes made or accounting entries made.

The best way to control these departments is to staff them with the right kind and caliber of personnel and equipment. While such "input controls" are important in any discretionary expense center, they are even more important when the process and outputs are undefined or difficult to measure.

To summarize, in computer services and accounting departments:

1. Develop *standards* if and where applicable.
2. Focus on *effectiveness* measures (timeliness of reports/services).
3. Emphasize making careful decisions about key *inputs* such as personnel and equipment.

The *personnel* department differs from the previous types of staff departments in that the appropriate focus of planning and control is on the process and workload rather than the inputs and outputs. The number and type of training and development activities conducted, the personnel reviews carried out, the recruiting and selection activities performed, grievances investigated and so on, can be planned and measured.

Standards may be applicable to certain routine activities, such as updating personnel files. To access the results and quality of these efforts is, however, difficult. Effectiveness measures that are of any practical significance tend to be indirect. For instance, training programs can be evaluated by the participants. But the true results show up only on the job and possibly much later.

To summarize, in the personnel department:

1. Develop *standards* if and where applicable.
2. Focus on *process* measures (workload).
3. Attempt to develop indirect or surrogate measures of *effectiveness* (unfilled positions, ratio of promotable to promoted, etc.).

Research and development departments for applied research, where specific results are expected within given deadlines, can be managed with the use of output and effectiveness measures. Project planning and control techniques are usually most appropriate.

Each research project or program should produce reports at specified intervals or when certain important events occur. These reports should include information about time spent, cost incurred and progress made.

In addition, these reports should include revised estimates of time and cost to complete the project. These updated estimates are vital in deciding whether to continue or drop the project.

If the research and development department engages in basic research, where the objective is to increase knowledge without any specific purpose in mind, project planning and control techniques have little value. The key decisions you need to make involve the amount of money to allocate to basic research (e.g., as a percent of sales) and to whom this money will be allocated. Essentially, input controls are all that are feasible.

To summarize, for research and development departments:

1. For applied research, use *project planning and control* techniques with regular reports that include revised estimates of additional time and costs to complete the projects.
2. For basic research, emphasize *input controls*.

For staff departments you should attempt to identify activities where standards can be applied and determine what combination of input, process/workload, output, effectiveness and efficiency measures are feasible.

In designing the budget formats for staff departments, you should apply the same step-by-step procedure recommended for production and marketing departments.

However, unlike production and marketing departments where the desired outputs (and in some cases, the process also) are clear-cut and measurable, the discretionary character of staff departments and the intangible nature of most of their outputs demand special planning and control techniques.

SPECIAL PLANNING AND CONTROL TECHNIQUES FOR STAFF DEPARTMENTS

The special techniques developed for discretionary expense centers are based on the fact that their inputs can be measured objectively and in monetary terms. Consequently, at a minimum it is possible to specify expense or "appropriation budgets" for these responsibility centers.

Appropriation budgets are spending limits specified for each of the accounts under which expenses incurred are recorded. For example, the personnel manager in GMC would be informed through the appropriations budget how much he could spend on salaries and wages, travel, supplies, etc.

In contrast to "performance budgets" (the flexible overhead budget for the production department is a good example) where inputs and outputs are linked through efficiency measures, appropriation budgets attempt to convert the plan for the responsibility center into a suitable expenditure level. No attempt is made to link inputs with desired outputs, unlike the case of engineered expense centers.

USING VARIOUS TYPES OF ANALYSES

Appropriation budgets must, however, reflect a plan and be based on some analysis of the operations of the responsibility center.

The simplest analysis is a comparison of the proposed spending levels with those budgeted and incurred in the previous year. Such *incremental analyses* are a simple but powerful tool to judge appropriate spending levels. If the personnel manager in GMC requests a substantial increase in his appropriation budget, he should be required to identify and justify the changes in activities that make the increase necessary.

The key assumption in such incremental analysis is that the level of spending in the previous year was appropriate. Consequently, it is necessary only to examine the proposed changes in spending levels and the reasons for these changes.

However, this assumption may be questionable. The previously approved spending levels may not be appropriate. Zero-based budgeting techniques that facilitate the analysis of the total budget rather than just the increases therefore become important.

The initial approach adopted by zero-based budgeting proponents has become known as "sunset analysis." Sunset analysis presumes that the responsibility center does not exist. Starting from this "zero-base," the functions that the responsibility center should serve are identified and a new responsibility center is designed to fulfill these functions.

Although sunset analyses are mandated for certain government agencies at intervals of five years, it is a difficult procedure to carry out.

Variations on this analytical technique have been developed, some of which are better suited to business firms.

VARIATIONS OF STANDARD ANALYSES

One successful variation is "sensitivity analysis." Here the manager of the responsibility center is asked what activities or functions will be affected, added or dropped if authorized spending levels are increased or decreased by 10, 15 or 20 percent.

Thus, the personnel manager at GMC might identify training programs that could be added or dropped if his budget changed. The general manager can then make a more meaningful judgment about the appropriate level of spending for the personnel department.

Another more comprehensive variation is the "decision-package" approach. The managers of responsibility centers are required to break down and group their activities into discrete, "stand-alone" packages. Each can be added or dropped without affecting the other packages. Though it demands greater effort during the first year, the decision-package approach usually justifies the added effort required.

IDENTIFYING STANDARD PROCEDURES

In addition to these analytical techniques, you may find it useful to review and specify, to the extent you can, standard operating procedures for discretionary expense centers.

A good example is the insurance company which employs mortgage examiners who normally review the legal aspects of mortgages being purchased from other financial institutions. When economic downturns reduce the number of mortgages offered for sale, it is standard operating practice for these mortgage examiners to shift to handling foreclosures, which increase during such economic conditions.

Another example could be in the personnel department in GMC, where clerical workers may be assigned to the accounting department for certain days at the beginning of each month to assist in the preparation of performance reports. The specification of standard operating procedures would ensure that the resources assigned to discretionary expense centers are employed more efficiently.

Another method to thoroughly explore but cautiously implement is the use of surrogate or indirect measures of effectiveness. The quality and availability of services that a particular responsibility center is expected to provide to other responsibility centers could, for instance, be assessed by the recipients. In particular, complaints about the availability and quality of service should be recorded and analyzed as a basis for improved planning and control of the operations of discretionary expense centers.

A further technique is the use of allocation techniques to cause an awareness and questioning of the cost of operating the firm's discretionary expense centers. An effective approach is to allocate the cost of each discretionary expense center to the responsibility centers receiving its services. If the amount of the personnel department's costs allocated to the manufacturing department increases for the coming budget year, compared to the allocation for the previous year, the manufacturing manager should raise questions. Such allocations ensure that the incremental analysis takes place effectively.

A precaution to be observed if allocation is adopted is to ensure that in performance reports the amount of allocation reported to, for instance, the manufacturing manager, should always be the same as the budgeted amount. Any variation between actual and budgeted amounts should not normally be considered the responsibility of the manufacturing manager. To report such variances in allocations would only result in wasted time and unnecessary explanations. The practice of allocations is useful when planning the budget, but is undesirable when comparing actual and budgeted performance.

PLANNING AND CONTROL FOCUS ON PERSONNEL

Many companies—Ford Motor Company is a particularly good example—focus on personnel as the key to planning and control for discretionary expense centers.

In most such responsibility centers, personnel is the single most important resource, sometimes involving 80% to 90% of costs. By carefully planning and strictly controlling the number and type of employees used by discretionary expense centers, firms can easily and effectively manage the level of expenses incurred by these centers. Thus, human resource management practices are an important determinant of the cost and quality of these staff departments.

These techniques all focus on internal company practices. Some companies use information from trade and industry associations to identify staff departments that merit careful analysis.

For example, if the accounting departments in firms similar to GMC employ, on the average, 6% of the personnel in the firms, and if GMC's accounting department employs 8%, then GMC should examine whether the difference is justified. Industry comparisons are useful but there might also be excellent reasons for a company to deviate from industry norms.

COMBINING STANDARDS AND SUPERVISION

Finally, discretionary expense centers in general, and staff departments in particular, almost always include activities where standards can be applied. It is worthwhile to seek out the activities that are in the nature of engineered expenses and develop standards that can serve as a basis for planning and control.

The techniques discussed above are effective. It is not desirable, though, to rely solely on such techniques to control the cost of staff departments or discretionary expense centers.

The managers of these staff departments must exercise close personal supervision over their subordinates. Also, the review of variances of actual costs and performance against budgeted costs and performance motivates the managers to pay close attention to their operations.

ACTION REQUIREMENTS

Carefully examine each of your staff departments to determine how they can best be planned and controlled. This determination may have been made earlier, when designing performance reports as recommended in Section III.

Given the disparities among staff departments, it is important to emphasize the careful selection of the appropriate planning and control focus from among the following:

1. Focus primarily on *effectiveness*. (Purchasing, computer services, accounting)

2. Focus primarily on *efficiency*. (Maintenance)

3. Focus primarily on the *workload* or *process*. (Personnel)

4. Focus on projects and *project planning and control* techniques. (Applied research and development)

5. Focus primarily on the *inputs* or *resources employed*. (Basic research, legal)

In addition to developing budget formats as recommended in previous sections, the range of techniques available for planning and controlling staff departments should be examined and suitable techniques selected for each one. These techniques include:

1. Using appropriation budgets.

2. Employing incremental analysis.

3. Applying "sunset analysis."

4. Trying "sensitivity analysis."

5. Identifying "decision packages."

6. Specifying standard operating procedures.

7. Developing surrogate/indirect measures of effectiveness.

8. Implementing allocation techniques.

9. Instituting suitable personnel practices.

10. Making industry comparisons.

11. Identifying engineered expense elements and applying standards.

VIII

Assessing Profit Potential
by Means of the Profit Budget

The profit budget is the primary focus of this book. The previous Sections provide the foundations on which to build the most effective profit budget.

The quality of the exercise used to develop the profit budget depends on the appropriateness of the definition of the firm's responsibility centers, the quality of its reporting system, the availability of standards of performance, and the design of the departmental/functional budgets.

In turn, it is important to realize that the profit budgeting process can greatly influence the quality of those departmental/functional budgets, performance standards and reporting systems. That process may even help identify shortcomings in the way responsibilities have been assigned to the departments.

PURPOSES OF THE PROFIT BUDGET

The design of the profit budgeting process and outputs is therefore vital to the effective management of the firm. The profit budget can and should serve a variety of purposes.

Profit Planning. This is the primary purpose of developing profit budgets. The profit budgeting exercise and documentation will be designed to focus on the identification and planned exploitation of the firm's profit potential.

Integration. The process of developing profit budgets is the mechanism by which the relationships between departmental/functional budgets are managed. The interaction of sales potential, production capacity, financial capabilities, personnel resources, and raw material availability should be explicitly considered in order to improve profits in line with the firm's business strategy.

Communication. The profit budgeting process brings about the integration of the departmental/functional budgets into the company's overall budgets by promoting communication within the firm. Those communication channels exist among the departments and hierarchical levels of management. You can obtain the desired nature and scope of the communication by suitably designing the profit budgeting process and documents.

Motivation and Control. The profit budgeting system can serve as a powerful mechanism to encourage and promote better managerial performance. You can design the budgeting process to allow appropriate participation of lower level managers in the determination of their goals. The greater the uncertainty, the more the complexity, and the higher the levels of managerial competence, the greater should be the degree and kind of participation in the budgeting process.

Setting challenging but not impossible goals can arouse managers' instincts for achievement. The logic and clarity of the action plans you set up to achieve such goals can promote better managerial understanding of what should be done in specific decision situations. The process of reviewing actual performance against budgeted expectations offers considerable opportunities for exercising control and improving the managerial climate in the firm.

OTHER BENEFITS OF THE PROFIT BUDGET

In addition to those four key purposes, the profit budget provides certain related benefits.

For one, the budgeting process can be used as a means to develop the analytical capabilities and broaden the perspectives and understanding of managers in the firm. It will also reveal instances of unclear or overlapping authority for decision-making, thus enabling you to create a more rational organizational structure.

In designing the profit budgeting system, the key purposes will determine appropriate design. However, the fringe benefits should also be sought as long as the design of a system that promotes such incidental benefits does not become too complex or conflict with the accomplishment of those primary purposes.

COMPONENTS OF THE PROFIT BUDGETING SYSTEM

In developing the best approach to the design of the profit budgeting system, it is necessary to break down the system into components. This simplifies the description of the system. The parts of the system (covered individually in subsequent Sections) are:

1. *The analytical process.* Focuses on what factors (the external environment, competition, past performance and internal capabilities) should be analyzed to identify the pockets of profit potential available to your company. Includes appropriate techniques to analyze these factors.

2. *The content of the budget.* Includes the quantitative goals, action plans and contingency plans that constitute the documentation of the profit budget. Discusses the key issue of how far into the future the profit budget should look.

3. *The process of development.* The relationship between the content of the budget and the analytical process to be used in arriving at it is fundamental. That content and process are tied together by suitably assigning the responsibilities for carrying out the analysis, and formulating and approving the budget documents.

4. *The performance review.* The activity that gives practical significance to the whole exercise is the review of actual performance against the budget. Involves the guidelines that ensure this review process is carried out effectively and with a positive impact on managerial motivation.

ANALYZING THE EXTERNAL ENVIRONMENT

A firm's profits derive from matching its capabilities with opportunities offered in the external environment. The effectiveness of the profit budget therefore depends on how well you analyze that environment and how well you identify your company's capabilities and limitations.

The key to analyzing the external environment effectively is to strike a balance between conducting too limited an analysis and wasting time and effort on irrelevant factors. While there is no guaranteed method to arrive at the appropriate level of comprehensiveness, a simple matrix is very valuable in guiding the depth and breadth of your analysis.

The range of external factors (other than competition, which we will discuss separately) that merit attention includes the following categories:

1. Economic forecasts
2. Technological changes
3. Regulatory factors
4. Social trends
5. Demographic trends
6. Political developments.

These factors can exist at a level of immediate relevance to your firm, at the level of the industry in which you operate, and at the level of the regions/country in which the firm does business. You must decide what levels are appropriate to your operation.

In the case of General Meters Corporation, all three levels are important. By combining the types of external factors and the levels at which they have relevance, you compile a matrix like the one illustrated in Figure 19.

The matrix is a simple but effective way to promote comprehensiveness in the identification of relevant external developments. Without this matrix, the identification and prioritization of environmental factors would be haphazard and potentially unsatisfactory.

First fill in your matrix with a very comprehensive identification of relevant factors. Once you complete this first assessment, carefully consider each factor to identify those that are likely to affect the firm's profits and those that require some action response. Then drop all other factors from further consideration.

ANALYZING YOUR COMPETITION

The most commonly held perception of a firm's competitors may be appropriate from the marketing manager's viewpoint, but not the general manager's. Most companies see their competitors as other firms that sell the same or similar products. Some firms go further. They include competitors who do not produce similar products, but compete for the same customer dollar.

That broader definition of competition would suggest that firms making giant screen television sets compete with firms that make above-ground swimming pools. A family that invests in one of these very dissimilar products probably will not be able or willing to buy the other for a significant period of time.

Product and market definitions of competition, however, are inadequate because they focus on only one of three possible dimensions of competition. These product-market based definitions recognize only the "output" dimensions of competition.

OTHER DIMENSIONS OF COMPETITION

A second and important dimension of competition is the "process" dimension. This is less obvious and relates to the nature of the technology employed by the company.

For example, two firms that produce hand-held calculators and missile guidance computers do not compete along the output or product-market dimension. However, both employ electronics technology and both may possess the competence to manufacture the other's products. Thus, firms that compete along the process or technology dimension could eventually compete along the output or product-market dimension.

Recognizing this technological dimension of competition is vital. Developments in technology can make a company's products obsolete. PP&G Industries experienced this traumatic situation when another firm developed float glass. Electronic facsimile transmission may make overnight letter delivery unnecessary.

The firm that identifies the potential sources of its obsolescence and exploits these sources is likely to survive and grow. If makers of wooden skis had foreseen the development of superior metal skis, they could have added them to their product lines. Similarly, the manufac-

MATRIX FOR ENVIRONMENTAL ANALYSIS GENERAL METERS CORPORATION

LEVELS

FACTORS	FIRM	INDUSTRY	REGIONAL	NATIONAL
Economic	Credit will be available but at 17% or higher interest rates.	Marginal firms likely to go bankrupt.	Southwest and West will experience significantly more investment in new plant than Northeast and Midwest.	Recession expected to continue. Interest rates will remain high. Housing starts will decline further. No increase in investment in new plants.
Technological	Local computer service bureau permits increased computer applications in manufacturing.	Electronic flow meters of improved performance characteristics and reduced cost are becoming available.	No significant regional differences.	Explosion in computer-aided design and manufacturing (CAD-CAM) capabilities.
Regulatory	Occupational safety regulations will be enforced.	No significant developments.	Pollution control emphasis likely to increase in West and Southwest.	Continued emphasis on health, environmental and safety standards.

LEVELS

FACTORS	FIRM	INDUSTRY	REGIONAL	NATIONAL
Social	Loyalty to company declining as alternative employment opportunities emerge.	Preference for high technology firms will affect new recruitment.	Movement away from single family housing to apartment complexes and condominiums.	Increased mobility, reduced commitment to traditional family structure.
Demographic	Percentage of elderly in local population will continue to increase.	No significant developments.	Movement of population from Northeast to Southwest and West.	Tendency toward zero population growth continues.
Political	Local taxes likely to increase to fund new welfare programs.	Industry association will open office in capital.	Investment incentives in Northeast will increase in response to movement of capital to Southwest and West.	New party in power will emphasize business and industry's role in national development.

Figure 19. Analysis of environment for General Meters Corporation

turers of metal skis should have anticipated and exploited the application of fiberglass and carbon technology in the manufacture of even better skis.

GMC must be sensitive to the development of more accurate, reliable and perhaps less expensive electronic flow meters. It should consider aggressively exploiting the developments in computer-aided design and computer-aided manufacture (CAD/CAM).

A THIRD COMPETITIVE DIMENSION

A third and equally important dimension of competition is the "input" or resources dimension. Firms that compete for finances from the same sources are excellent examples. They could be in totally different industries and employ different technologies. Yet they may compete for the same managerial, labor and financial resources.

Any firm that competes successfully along the input/resource dimension is also well-situated to initiate more direct competition along the process-technology and output-product-market dimensions. Apart from that potential threat, companies that have to accept resources of lesser magnitude or poorer quality might plunge into a declining spiral leading to reduced profits and possible extinction.

IDENTIFYING COMPETITORS BY DIMENSION

The first step in analyzing competition is to identify your three or four most important competitors in relation to each of those three dimensions. Too many competitors makes the analysis too demanding and perhaps superficial. Too few could result in overlooking important insights. After selecting approximately 10 to 12 firms, you can conduct an in-depth analysis which should include both the traditional financial analysis as well as a more qualitative examination.

CONDUCTING A FINANCIAL ANALYSIS

The conventional analysis of published or available financial statements of the competitors is the first step. It is essential that you examine trends in financial figures and ratios over a period of at least three years in order to develop a meaningful appreciation of competitors' perform-ances. Figure 20 lists key figures and ratios.

Most of the ratios and numbers included in Figure 20 are well-known and need no explanation. Several are relatively uncommon.

For example, the ratio of capital expenditures to depreciation suggests how much importance the firm's management places on main-taining or improving productive capacity. Also, the ratio of net fixed assets to gross fixed assets is a measure of how modern or recent the company's plant and equipment are.

FINANCIAL ANALYSIS OF COMPETITION

1. Profits—growth rate
2. Earnings per share—growth rate
3. Sales—growth rate
4. Profits/sales
5. Sales/capital employed (equity + long-term debt)
6. Profits/capital employed
7. Profits/labor costs (or number of employees)
8. Net fixed assets/number of employees
9. Sales/number of employees
10. Sales/inventories
11. Accounts receivable as days of sales
12. Current assets/current liabilities
13. (Cash + marketable securities + receivables)/current liabilities
14. Long-term debt/equity
15. Total debt/total assets
16. Research & development expenses/sales
17. Sources and uses of funds
18. Capital expenditures/depreciation
19. Net fixed assets/gross fixed assets

Figure 20. Key numbers and ratios for financial analysis of competitors

CONDUCTING A QUALITATIVE ANALYSIS

Employees of your firm who have direct or indirect contacts with competitive firms are prime sources of qualitative information.

Field sales personnel can obtain information about competitive activities from distributors or customers who have dealings with those competitors. Manufacturing and R&D personnel may interact with competitors' personnel at professional meetings or conventions.

In addition, all publications of the competitors—annual reports, press releases, price lists, brochures, in-house newsletters and even advertisements—can provide signals about competitive intentions. Sales and distribution practices, credit policies, product development in progress, pricing policies, and personnel and hiring practices, are all areas of importance in the competitive arena.

You may find it necessary to designate specific individuals to collect, filter and disseminate information about competitors. Over a period of time, these individuals will surely develop valuable sources and insights about those selected competitors.

IMPORTANCE

		HIGH	LOW
I M M I	IMMEDIATE ACTION REQUIRED	High (17%) borrowing rate. Electronic flow meters being offered by competition.	Local taxes likely to increase. Industry association location in capital.
N E N C E	DELAYED RESPONSE ADEQUATE	Computer service bureau facilities improvement. CAD/CAM applications increasing. Political climate increasingly favorable to business.	Increasing proportion of elderly in local population. Loyalty of employees declining. Investment incentives in Northeast likely to increase.

Table 6. Sample categorization of environmental and competitive issues

UTILIZING THE EXTERNAL ANALYSES

Studying the external environmental factors and competition should result in a list of practical "issues."

For example, each of the cells in the matrix in Figure 19 which contains relevant environmental developments will have implications for GMC. The availability of credit, but at high interest rates, might indicate the need to postpone capital expenditures and trim working capital. The increase in CAD/CAM applications nationwide might suggest that GMC should investigate possibilities in that area. The expected increase in local taxes means that cash flow and profit estimates must be suitably adjusted.

A useful technique for classifying the issues identified is to categorize them into four groups like those in Table 6.

CLASSIFYING THE ISSUES

The four-way classification in Table 6 ranges from important issues that require immediate action to unimportant issues that do not require an immediate response. This classification offers two benefits. First, it prioritizes the issues and enables managers to focus on those that require swift response. Second, it facilitates the identification of patterns that lead to the development of scenarios used to guide profit budgets.

For example, the development of electronic flow meters by the competition is critical for GMC management. R&D projects may have to be initiated immediately develop GMC's own line of electronic meters. Alternatively, technical collaboration might be sought.

The major growth markets are likely to be in the Southwest and West and logistics may dictate that a new plant be located in the West. At the same time, the combination of tight money and the investment incentives likely to be offered by the Northeastern region are highly attractive when considered with the economies of scale and management cohesion resulting from expanding the present facilities.

The key assumptions and variables are the in-house development or purchase of electronics technology, the continuation of the tight money situation and the likelihood and magnitude of investment incentives in the Northeast. With a different set of assumptions, GMC might decide to continue with its present mechanical meters or invest in a new plant in the West.

Different scenarios can be developed by varying the assumptions within reasonable limits. These alternative scenarios should be detailed, with the most likely one identified as a basis for General Meters management's decision-making.

Such scenarios will also produce an improved classification of the issues. For instance, investment incentives in the Northeast, which originally had been classified as unimportant, become a significant issue as the pattern of relationships among the issues emerges.

The Importance-Imminence Matrix in Table 6 and the development of scenarios will help you prioritize the issues identified and highlight their patterns or interrelationships. However, the analysis and its integration are incomplete without consideration of the abilities and limitations of the company itself.

FINANCIAL ANALYSIS OF YOUR OWN COMPANY

You can divide the internal situation of the company into two components. First, the past performance, accomplishments and failures of the firm must be understood so you can better predict and influence the future. Second, the current core skills, distinctive competences and key shortcomings of the firm must be comprehensively identified to permit exploiting the strengths and remedying the weaknesses.

The initial step in understanding the past is to conduct a detailed financial analysis. Much more information should be available about your own company than about its competition. Consequently, a more thorough analysis is feasible than that in Figure 20. The analyses you'll need are listed in Figure 21.

The trends indicated by such analyses are the key pieces of information. Trends that are at variance with expectations or are out of line with the other numbers should receive particular attention.

THE ANALYTICAL PROCESS: A MANAGERIAL AUDIT

The second step in analyzing the internal situation is to identify the core skills, distinctive competences and key shortcomings of the firm. What

FINANCIAL ANALYSIS OF THE FIRM

1. Profits—growth rate
2. Earnings per share—growth rate
3. Sales—growth rate
4. Profits/sales
5. Sales/capital employed (equity + long-term debt)
6. Profits/capital employed
7. Sales growth rate/market growth rate
8. Profits/labor costs
9. Profits/number of employees
10. Net fixed assets/number of employees
11. Sales/number of employees
12. Sales/inventories
13. Accounts receivable as days of sales
14. Current assets/current liabilities
15. (Cash + marketable securities + receivables)/current liabilities
16. Long-term debt/equity
17. Total debt/total assets
18. Research & development expenses/sales
19. Sources and uses of funds
20. Capital expenditure/depreciation
21. Net fixed assets/gross fixed assets
22. Cost of goods sold as % of sales
23. Material costs as % of sales
24. Labor cost as % of sales
25. Rate of change in prices
26. Product mix changes—total and by region
27. Proportion of capital expenditures allocated to each department—trend
28. Market share by product line and region—trend

Figure 21. Key figures and ratios for financial analysis of your own firm

has the firm relied on as its primary strength in making profits? What does the firm do better than its competitors? What are its principal weaknesses?

You will need to focus on several aspects of this mainly qualitative analysis. First, much of the information that affords useful insights may be in the form of anecdotes or stories about particular experiences. Such information should be handled carefully. In such instances it is useful to choose two extreme experiences or perceptions relating to the issue. Then identify what made the two instances different.

For example, a firm that utilized teams of executives to develop operating plans for its product lines studied the experiences of the most conspicuously successful team in comparison with a less successful team. It then developed guidelines to improve the effectiveness of its management teams. Those guidelines included clear-cut directions for improvements relating to the process followed, the involvement of senior management, the definition of the responsibilities of the teams, and so on. Studying just one experience would not have been as successful and could have resulted in a biased understanding.

Second, a company's management systems should be a major part of the study. It is not uncommon to find managerial audits focusing primarily (if not solely) on tangible areas, such as products, markets, distribution channels and manufacturing capabilities.

Third, it may be desirable to assign responsibility for such analyses to individuals who are not defensive about the past or about the status quo. If you are studying manufacturing, you may want to employ sources other than, or in addition to, the manufacturing manager. Often managers of departments or functions who have close interactions with the department or function being studied will have useful insights to offer.

Fourth, and of particular importance, strengths and weaknesses of a firm often can be assessed only in relation to environmental opportunities and threats. For instance, at GMC, the lack of design and manufacturing competence for electronic flow meters will not show up as a weakness without the recognition of the development of these products by competitors. Also, what is a strength (location in the Northeast) in one scenario (attractive investment incentives in the Northeast) may be a weakness in the context of another scenario (setting up a plant in the Southwest).

The managerial audit should expressly address the topics listed in Table 7.

1. Organizational structure
   Appropriateness of responsibility centers
   Allocation of responsibility and authority

2. Planning and control systems
   Long-range or strategic planning
   Budgeting
   Reporting
   Review and follow-up
   Transfer pricing
   Materials, production
   Accounting, billing

3. Policies
   Personnel
   Credit
   Research & Development
   Product
   Customer service

4. Marketing
   Pricing
   Products
   Advertising
   Market research
   Distribution
   Inventories

5. Manufacturing
   Production planning and control
   Inventories
   Maintenance
   Capacity utilization (bottleneck areas)
   Human resources
   Product diversification capabilities

6. Personnel
   Recruitment and selection
   Training and development
   Records management

Table 7. Targets for an internal management audit

7. Finance
   Sources and uses of funds
   Relationships with sources
   Cash management
8. Research & development
   Investment
   Success rate, impact
   Human resources
9. Management
   Climate
   Competence, capabilities
   Turnover
   Age, experience
   Second line development

Table 7. Continued

INTEGRATING THE INTERNAL ANALYSES

Following the financial analysis and managerial audit, you then must assimilate and integrate the findings of these internal activities. Two considerations should guide your integration. The first consideration involves seeking the *distinctive competences* of the firm. What capabilities does the firm possess which give it an edge over its competition? Broadly speaking, that competitive edge can be in terms of:

- Facilities
- Access to Markets (Distribution Channels)
- Access to Raw Materials
- Labor Availability and Cost
- Finance (Magnitude and Cost)
- Technology
- Management (Personnel and Systems).

The second consideration is *consistency*. Has there been consistency over time in the allocation of capital funds to departments and functions? Are those departments and functions set up to be consistent with each other's capabilities and requirements? (For example, are the distribution and warehousing practices consistent with the single plant situation at GMC?) Has the distinctive competence remained the same or has it changed in terms of nature or magnitude?

The identification of distinctive competences will influence the selection of environmental opportunities for exploitation. For example, at GMC, if finance is its distinctive competence, perhaps the electronic flow meter product should be aggressively developed and marketed immediately without waiting for an economic upturn, in order to build market share before competition becomes severe. If manufacturing in terms of costs and technology for the existing electro-mechanical product lines is GMC's distinctive competence, then perhaps it should prepare to compete on price to maintain or increase its share of a possibly declining market.

The inconsistencies uncovered also will direct managerial action through the profit budgeting system. Perhaps GMC has ignored or inadequately developed the abililty to service existing customers if they have problems following installation of GMC's meters. Or the key to gaining market share in a situation where competitive products are similar in quality and prices may be to offer better after-sales service to industrial customers.

As another example, the location of the single GMC manufacturing facility in the Northeast may emerge as inconsistent with the growth markets of the Southwest and West. Perhaps there is need to explore the economics of regional warehouses (for standard products and parts) or even a new manufacturing facility in the West.

Figure 22 graphically illustrates an overview of the recommended internal and external analyses.

ACTION REQUIREMENTS

The action requirements relating to this Section are described at the end of Section X because of the close relationship of Sections VIII, IX and X. For instance, the issue of how far into the future the profit budget should cover is discussed in Section IX, and this decision has particular implications for the external analyses.

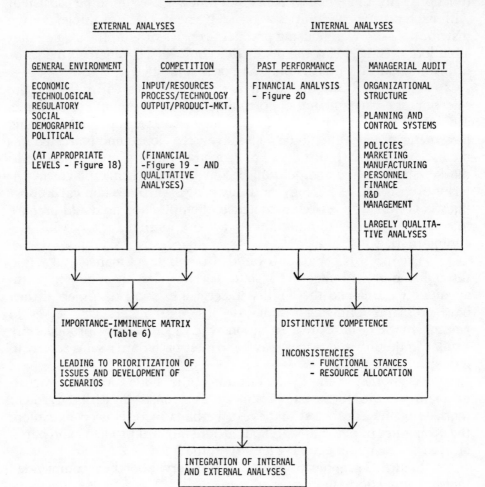

Figure 22. An overview of the internal and external analyses

Also, the decisions regarding who should be assigned responsibility for the recommended analyses are covered in Section X. Unless these decisions are made, no action can be taken on the analyses recommended in this Section. Keep in mind the focus and scope of the analyses recommended so far when you study the next two Sections.

IX

The Profit Budget—
Forging the Action Plan

There are two characteristics in particular that distinguish the profit budget recommended here from the conventional budgets developed in most firms.

First, the time horizon (number of years into the futures) that the profit budget is designed to cover must be carefully selected according to the characteristics of each firm. The conventional choice of a one-year or two-year horizon is essentially arbitrary and stems from the traditional financial emphasis of budgets. The one-year horizon undesirably reinforces the financial orientation of the budget, unless a one-year horizon truly reflects the operating characteristics of the firm.

The action orientation of our profit budgeting system requires that the choice of the time horizon be consistent with the nature of the actions and decisions typical of your individual firm.

ANOTHER DIFFERENCE BETWEEN SYSTEMS

The second major difference between the proposed profit budgeting system and conventional budgets is the scope and focus of the content of the profit budgeting system.

Traditional budgets focus on financial statements. The proposed system will focus on *action plans* that are carefully and logically developed to be consistent with the environmental opportunities and internal capabilities of the firm. The quantitative goals employed to define the firm's direction and measure its accomplishments will include both financial and non-financial performance indicators.

In addition, in the light of the range of uncertainties that have an impact on a firm's performance, suitable *contingency plans* will be included as part of the documentation of the profit budget.

DETERMINING THE BUDGET HORIZON

Your profit budget must respond to the nature of your firm's activities. Each firm usually has an obvious operating cycle if all its products belong to a single industry. An operating cycle is the length of time it takes to manufacture and sell a typical product.

In the garment industry, operating cycles cannot exceed six months because of the influence of fashion and seasonal changes. In the shipbuilding industry, the operating cycle is normally two to three years. In many manufacturing firms, the operating cycle is less than a year.

Table 8 shows how the profit budget must be linked to the operating cycle.

The reasoning behind the recommended time horizons in Table 8 is simple. The time horizon of the profit budget cannot be less than one year, regardless of how short the operating cycle is. You need fore-

PROFIT BUDGET TIME HORIZON AND THE OPERATING CYCLE

OPERATING CYCLE	RECOMMENDED TIME HORIZON
Less than 6 months	1 year
6 months to 1 year	2 years
More than 1 year but less than 2 years	3 years
More than 2 years	Operating cycle plus 1 year rounded upwards to the nearest whole number. (e.g.: 2.4 year operating cycle + 1 year = 4 year time horizon.)

Table 8. The profit budget horizon and the operating cycle

casted financial statements of at least one year to plan cash management, negotiate with financing agencies and unions, and so forth. The financial community operates on an annual cycle and the firm has no option but to comply with this convention.

Assuming that profit budgets are rolling plans developed on an annual basis, the time horizon should be designed to capture the implications of managerial actions and decisions taken toward the end of the budget year. That creates the need to add one year to the operating cycle to determine the budget time horizon.

Because it is difficult to work with periods less than a year, the time horizon is always specified in whole numbers. This practice of using whole numbers of years also fits in with an annual update of the profit budget.

INCORPORATING CONSEQUENCES INTO THE TIME HORIZON

The key consideration in determining the time horizon is that it should be long enough to encompass the consequences of the operating decisions and actions of managers. This is the reason the operating cycle has such a major influence on the recommended time horizon. In addition to the operating cycle, you may find it useful to identify key decisions made by operating managers, and examine the normal time period it takes for the results of those operating decisions to show up.

For instance, in a firm that relies primarily on advertising to generate sales, the budget horizon should encompass the period over which advertisements are expected to measurably influence sales. Examples of such firms are those whose products are discretionary or luxury purchases, such as toys and cosmetics.

Some firms emphasize new product development as an operational rather than strategic responsibility. In the breakfast food industry, particularly the segment focusing on children, new products and packaging must constantly be developed and phased out. In such cases the determination of the operating cycle should take new product development times into account. The profit budget time horizon should encompass the period over which operating actions and decisions will have a measurable impact on the firm's performance.

The argument that the degree of uncertainty affecting the firm should also influence the time horizon of budgets is tenuous, at best. Regardless of uncertainties, managers have to make decisions and take actions. The best estimate of the impact of these decisions and actions has to be made based on the current understanding of what is most likely to happen. If assumptions about the future prove wrong, it is the role of contingency plans to respond to these developments.

OPERATING CYCLES AT GENERAL METERS

Applying the above recommendations to GMC, it appears that the two product lines—residential and industrial—have different operating cycles.

In the residential product line, manufacturing and selling are parallel processes. Thus, the operating cycle for residential products probably equals the normal manufacturing time for the standard residential meters.

In the industrial product line, order generation and manufacture are sequential processes, since the meters are largely made to order. The operating cycle is therefore the sum of the times it normally takes to generate an order and to manufacture the product.

Advertising is maintained at a constant level. So the impact of advertising decisions is likely to be constant and can be ignored. New product development is not a significant activity, and hence has little bearing on the time horizon.

It would seem that the sum of the order generating plus manufacturing times of the industrial product line should be the operating cycle that determines the time horizon GMC's profit budget. The operating cycle of the residential product line is shorter. If the time horizon were determined on that basis, it would be too short for the industrial product line. In cases such as GMC where more than one operating cycle exists, the longest should be chosen to determine the budget horizon (unless the shorter is a very important product).

The operating cycle of GMC's industrial product line normally lies between six months and one year. According to Table 8, the time horizon of GMC's profit budget should be two years.

EIGHT STEPS TO FORMULATING THE PROFIT BUDGET

The analyses of the external environment and internal capabilities of the firm, discussed in Section VIII, must be integrated into the statement of the profit budget.

In compiling the analyses of opportunities and capabilities, you should recall the desired outputs of action plans, quantitative goods and contingency plans.

Here is the recommended sequence.

1. List the external issues identified as very important and requiring immediate response next to the distinctive competences and inconsistencies identified by the internal analysis.

2. Compile external issues and related distinctive competences and inconsistencies to identify opportunities in line with distinctive competences (strengths) and threats that appear to aggravate the inconsistencies (weaknesses).

3. Develop alternative action plans for each matched set of opportunities/strengths, and threats/weaknesses. Use the analysis of competition as one of the bases for identifying alternatives.

4. Identify the key dimensions which distinquish the alternatives generated for each set.

5. Classify the alternatives generated for each set along the dimensions identified above.

6. Develop a comprehensive, skeleton action plan by selecting one alternative from each set of strengths/opportunities and threats/weaknesses. The selected alternatives should be as mutually consistent as possible in relation to the key dimensions identified in Step 4; in keeping with the most likely environmental scenario developed by using the Importance-Imminence Matrix; and conform to top management's preferences.

7. Repeat Steps 1 through 6 for issues classified as important but requiring only a delayed response.

8. Identify the expected financial and physical consequences of the selected action plan. If more than one action plan appears desirable, employ such consequences to select the best from among the acceptable plans.

ASSESSING THE ISSUES AT GMC

The next few pages illustrate the recommended sequence for profit budget development at GMC. Table 6 in Section VIII identified the following external issues as important to GMC:

1. High borrowing rate (immediate).
2. Electronic flow meters being offered by competition (immediate).
3. Computer service bureau offering improved facilities.
4. CAD/CAM applications increasing.
5. Political climate increasingly favorable.
6. Investment incentives likely in the Northeast. (Identified as important following development of scenarios.)

The most likely environmental scenario—identified on the basis of the Importance-Imminence Matrix—was:

- High borrowing rates likely to continue
- Investment incentives in the Northeast likely to be offered within the next year
- Growth of industries and housing will be mainly in the Southwest and West
- Competition will change in that there will be fewer but stronger competitors
- The political climate will probably be more positive toward the needs of business and industry.

The distinctive competences and inconsistencies that would result from the recommended internal analysis would probably include the following:

A. Distinctive competences
1. Management experience and familiarity with existing product line and manufacturing technology.
2. Excellent distribution channels for residential products.
3. Highly efficient manufacturing processes with large proportion of specialized equipment.
4. Excellent relationship with financing institutions.
5. Five-year record of profitability and growth higher than industry average.

B. Inconsistencies

1. Aging workforce with increasing shortages of skilled machinists.
2. Single plant location in Norhteast with growth markets in the Southwest and West.
3. No significant computer or electronics capabilities among present employees.
4. Excessive reliance on management experience because of inadequate formal planning and control systems.

Based on the preceding results of the internal and external analyses, Figure 23 takes you through the steps of developing the action plan.

Step 1. Listing of important and immediate issues, distinctive competences and inconsistencies.

Issues	*Distinctive Competences*
High borrowing rate	Management experience
Electronic flow meters being offered	Excellent distribution
	Efficient manufacturing
	Excellent financial relationships
	Five-year record of profitability
	Inconsistencies
	Aging workforce
	Single plant location
	No computer/electronics capability
	Ineffective formal planning and control

Step 2. Matching issues with competences and inconsistencies.

Set A. High borrowing rate	Excellent financial relationships Five-year record of profitability
Set B. Electronic flow meters being offered	No computer/electronics capability

Figure 23. Applying the profit budget development steps at GMC

Step 3. Developing alternative action plans.

Set A:

Alternative 1.   Postpone all borrowing until interest rates decline. Selectively reduce working capital. Postpone capital expenditures.

Alternative 2.   Utilize excellent relationships and excellent profit record to negotiate additional, relatively favorable lines of credit. Offer generous credit terms to customers. Improve delivery times and service by increasing inventories of standard meters and parts. Invest in added plant capacity if needed to seize market share lost by bankrupt competitors and taken away from less financially viable competitors.

Set B:

Alternative 1.   Continue existing line of mechanical meters. Utilize experience and manufacturing efficiency to remain profitable even if total market demand declines.

Alternative 2.   Recruit personnel from competitors who possess needed electronics knowledge. Add appropriate facilities in Northeast, utilizing expected investment incentives.

Alternative 3.   Recruit personnel from competitors who possess needed electronics knowledge. Invest in new plant in West to manufacture electronic meters. Strengthen formal planning and control systems.

Step 4. Identifying key dimensions of differences between alternatives.

Set A:

Financial policy	Conservative	⟷	Aggressive
Growth orientation	Status quo	⟷	High growth
Profit orientation	Short-term	⟷	Long-term
Risk	Low	⟷	High

Figure 23. Continued

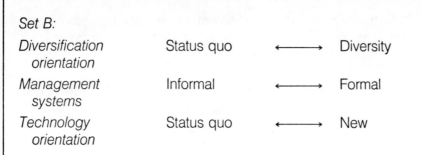

Set B:

Diversification orientation	Status quo	⟷	Diversity
Management systems	Informal	⟷	Formal
Technology orientation	Status quo	⟷	New

Step 5. Classifying alternatives.

	Alternatives				
	Set A		Set B		
Dimensions	1	2	1	2	3
Profit orientation	Short term	Long term	Short term	Long term	Long term
Growth orientation	Status quo	High growth	Status quo	High growth	High growth
Diversification orientation	Status quo	Status quo	Status quo	Diversify	Diversify
Management systems	Informal	Informal	Informal	Informal	Formal
Financial policy	Conservative	Aggressive	Conservative	Less Conservative	Aggressive
Technology orientation	Status quo	Status quo	Status quo	New	New
Risk	Low	High	Low	Medium	High

Step 6. Developing a comprehensive action plan.

Assuming a conservative top management and ownership and a long recessionary period, a consistent action plan would be to implement alternatives A1 and B1. Such an action plan would focus on reducing borrowings by lowering working capital. (Extreme care must be taken in any efforts aimed at asset reduction.) Also, manufacturing efficiencies would be emphasized to increase the profitability margins of existing products and compete, if necessary, in terms of price.

Figure 23. Continued

Step 7. Repeating the process for less immediate issues.
This step is not presented here as it is not necessary for purposes of clarifying the process.

Step 8. Identifying expected financial and physical consequences.
Physical: Inventories of finished goods to be reduced by 10% in six months and 15% in 12 months.

Inventories of raw materials to be reduced by 10% in three months.

Working capital to be reduced by 10% in 12 months.

Manufacturing costs to be reduced by 5% across all product lines through reduced waste; to be accomplished in six months.

Product redesign and value engineering to reduce manufacturing costs by additional 10% in standard product lines.

Financial: Interest expense for the first year of the budget to be $12,000 less than previous year, and $15,000 less for the second year.

Profits to increase by $75,000 (on last year's volume of sales) for the first year of the budget, and by $100,000 (assuming no volume change) in the second year of the budget.

Figure 23. Continued

ADDITIONAL REQUIREMENTS FOR BUDGET DEVELOPMENT

Several points should be made with regard to the recommended sequence of steps for translating the analyses described in Section VIII into an integrated plan of action.

First, you must remain sensitive and flexible to the need to change initial perceptions and classifications. Just as it was found appropriate when developing scenarios to move the investment incentives in the Northeast to a more important cell in the classification matrix, you'll find it necessary to rework or add to the previous steps.

For example, you can now see the need to include the expected high growth in the Southwest and West as an important issue because of the debate about plant location. Such changes are inevitable and are usually indicative of a broadening or more realistic perspective, rather than poor initial analysis.

Second, you can accomplish Step 5 in a slightly different manner—if you need greater fineness in classification and greater visual impact—by profiling the alternatives as illustrated in Figure 24.

Third, the dimensions selected for classifying or profiling the alternatives depend on the nature of the business and the types of alternatives considered.

Normally you'd expect to find profit orientation, growth orientation, and risk among the dimensions selected. An obvious dimension that is not included in the illustration is profits or profitability. We recommend that you calculate the profitability of the alternatives later, after a coherent action plan is developed.

Too often, profitability calculations delay the analysis. Plus they

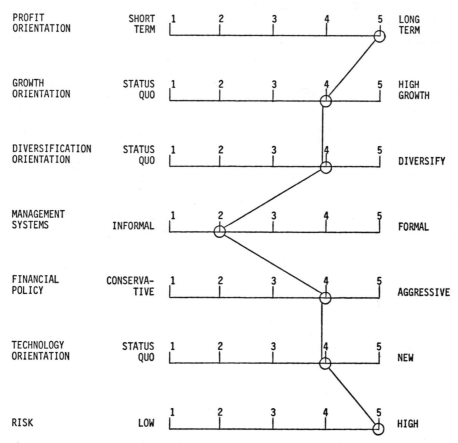

Figure 24. A profile of GMC's alternative B2

are subject to a whole series of assumptions which must be clarified before meaningful figures, such as those listed under Step 8 of the example, can be generated. The profitability calculations are best made after Step 7. If necessary, the action plan can be reworked with the addition of that profitability dimension.

Fourth, if you can identify several consistent combinations of alternatives in Step 6, the expected profitability of each consistent set can be a basis for selection of the best action plan.

Fifth, following the creation of an outlined action plan, it should be filled out with details such as the timing of actions, and responsibility for the execution and monitoring of the plan.

The expected financial and physical consequences developed as part of Step 8 constitute part of the quantititive goals that would form the basis for monitoring the effectiveness of the action plan and making needed changes.

STATING THE ACTION PLAN

The action plan developed is recorded as part of the budgets which are the responsibility of the managers who have to implement the plan.

For instance, the actions relating to manufacturing efficiency will be included on the second page of Figure 15 in Section V to the extent that the foreman of the Machine Shop is responsible for achieving progress toward the quantitative goals. The budget document for the general manager will incorporate those actions which he has the responsibility to execute or monitor.

We cannot overemphasize the importance of the action plan and the analytical process leading to its development as the crux of the entire profit budgeting system.

First, the analytical process ensures the kind of thinking and exploration built into the design of the budget formats for managers at levels below the general manager. The identification and matching of environmental potential with corporate capabilities is the key to optimizing profits. Thus, without the action planning process, it would be incorrect to argue that a budgeting system is effectively accomplishing the purpose of *profit planning*.

Second, the action plan delineates what needs to be done differently from the way operations are currently carried out. This contributes to the *communication* among departments and hierarchical levels needed to accomplish the integration which is basic to the budgeting system.

The various departments or responsibility centers can explicitly identify the changes in the support of, or relationships with, other departments or responsibility centers that should take place during the budget period. A budgeting system with a primarily financial orientation cannot be as effective in this regard.

Third, when comparing actual to budgeted performance during the review and follow-up process, the action plan greatly facilitates the identification of needed remedial action. The explicit assignment of responsibility for implementation and for monitoring the implementation contributes greatly to motivation. In addition, it simplifies the exercise of *control* because the timing and consequences of actions are specified so that you can determine whether the planned action was appropriate or not.

STATING THE QUANTITATIVE GOALS

Step 8 of the profit budget development process identifies the qualitative goals that result from the action plan. These goals are part of the plans for all managers who have any responsibility for executing or monitoring such an action plan.

Other quantitative goals for the firm as a whole flow naturally from the performance report designed for the general manager. The key indicators of performance relating to the managers reporting to him would be included in the performance report along with appropriate expectations.

In addition to these quantitative factors, you'll need to develop a projected cash flow statement for the budget period. That statement would normally be part of the performance report and budget format of the executive in charge of the finance function. In GMC, this would be the chief accountant.

Because of the cruical importance of cash management, the cash flow statement should also be include in the performance report and budget format of the chief executive. In GMC, the general manager-chief executive should receive monthly or weekly statements of the cash position and also have the projected cash flow statement as part of his budget documentation.

In most cases, experience dictates that you generate complete pro-forma financial statements (income statement and balance sheet) for the budget period. These pro-forma financial statements are necessary in the course of negotiations with external or non-management entities, such as banks and unions.

It would be inappropriate to use the general manager's performance report and related budget formats in such discussions—for obvious reasons. If these external requirements were not present, the statement of quantitative goals for the general manager (i.e., the firm as a whole) would be in those formats discussed in Section V.

FINANCIAL VS. NON-FINANCIAL GOALS

Before concluding the discussion of goals, consider the need to emphasize non-financial or physical goals in addition to financial goals. The ultimate, "bottom-line" financial measure or goal is profit. While it is understandably the single most important measure of performance, it does suffer from a variety of shortcomings.

First, it is possible for a firm to have objectives other than *just* profits. Maintaining employment levels, playing a major role in community affairs, being the acknowledged technological innovator in the industry or similar objectives may be of considerable importance to certain firms. These objectives are best measured in non-financial terms and should occupy a legitimate place in performance reports and budget formats.

Second, profit is essentially a short-term measure. It is possible to increase this year's profits by taking actions such as reducing corporate advertising, cutting down on management development, minimizing R&D expenses and so forth. However, such actions essentially exchange future profits for more profits in the present. To emphasize and understand the long-term implications of profit-maximizing decisions, non-financial measures such as market share and rate of new product development are essential.

Third, profits are affected by a variety of factors that may or may not be subject to the control of the firm's management. If they are not, it is desirable to employ other measures to help assess how much of the change in profits was due to managerial efforts and how much to chance.

Indicators such as market share and workload measures are valuable in this regard.

Fourth, profits are subject to manipulation within the bounds of generally accepted accounting principles. Non-financial measures can shed light on performance unaffected by accounting phenomena such as the effect of inventory fluctuations in a full costing system, and the effect of changes in accounting practices.

STATING CONTINGENCY PLANS

There are two distinctly different types of contingency plans, and each is effective in particular circumstances. The two approaches will be referred to as the "thermostat" (or "trigger variable") approach and the "scenario" approach. Table 9 shows the basic differences between these two approaches.

The simpler type of contingency plan (thermostat) is one that focuses on a single variable that is largely internal, such as sales or orders booked. It broadly outlines the actions to be taken when various situations arise—for example, sales or orders booked falling 10% below budgeted levels for two months in a row, or by 20% for one month, and so forth. A classic contingency plan of this type is the flexible budget employed in the manufacturing context and described in Section V.

	NUMBER OF VARIABLES CONSIDERED	
	SINGLE	MULTIPLE
INTERNAL	"THERMOSTAT" OR "TRIGGER VARIABLE" APPROACH	(NOT COMMONLY ADOPTED)
EXTERNAL	(NOT COMMONLY ADOPTED)	"SCENARIO" APPROACH

FOCUS OF VARIABLES CONSIDERED

Table 9. Comparison of two types of contingency plans

While such plans do possess the advantages of simplicity, ease of development and precise identification of responses, they are best suited to firms operating in relatively less complex and less uncertain environments. The Coca-Cola Company or McDonald's food chain could justifiably and effectively employ the thermostat type of contingency plan because of their simple, limited product lines and relatively few external variables of short-term importance.

For instance, Coca-Cola Company's sales of soft drinks within a budgeting period would probably be more affected by weather conditions than any other external factor. More complex firms operating in more complex environments should use the scenario approach, although the thermostat approach could still be used for responsibility centers within those firms.

SCENARIO CONTINGENCY PLANS

The scenario approach focuses on several external variables that describe the relevant environment for the firm. At GMC, the following variables would be important:

1. Housing starts by region.
2. New investments in process plants by region.
3. Market share of firms in meter industry that will go bankrupt.
4. Prime lending rate.
5. Inflation rate.
6. Expected price changes for major raw materials.
7. Market share captured by electronic meters.

For each of the selected variables, the most likely value or state during the budget period is decided. This will be the scenario on which the detailed action plan is developed in the initial budget formation process

At the same time, the most unfavorable value or state and the most favorable value or state that can reasonably (5% to 10% probability) be expected during the budget period are identified for each variable.

These two values or states for each variable give rise to two additional scenarios, the most pessimistic and the most optimistic. For each of these two scenarios, you should develop outlines of action plans. These broad action plans constitute the contingency plans for your firm.

This approach to contingency planning has advantages and disadvantages. Its primary advantage is that it focuses management attention on variables that, though largely out of its control, will have a significant impact on the firm. It forces management to analyze in advance the complex implications of variations in these factors. In comparison, the thermostat approach might contribute to managerial insensitivity to important external developments.

The complexity of the exercise is a disadvantage. Another disadvantage is that the actual situation that develops will probably not coincide with any of the three (most pessimistic, most likely, and most optimistic) scenarios.

Also, certain variables may move toward the pessimistic end and others toward the optimistic end. Management, therefore, cannot strictly apply the contingency plans developed for the pessimistic or optimistic scenarios. Sound judgment is required to determine the appropriate response to the actual development.

In our experience the advantages of the scenario approach to contingency planning significantly outweigh the disadvantages. The more effective identification of the need to modify the action plan is very valuable.

In addition, if you pay adequate attention and thought to the develpment of the contingency plans for the pessimistic and optimistic scenarios, you'll develop a valuable appreciation of the range of alternative responses that should be considered. As a consequence, the speed and effectiveness with which responses to unanticipated developments are implemented is greatly enhanced.

ACTION REQUIREMENTS

As mentioned in the previous Section, the action requirements for this Section will be described following Section X which focuses on the assignment of responsibility for developing the profit budget. The action requirements for this Section are best considered following the discussion of how and to whom to assign responsibility for the recommended analyses.

X

Managing the Process of Profit Budget Development

The two previous Sections covered the required process of analysis and the desired output of the profit budget. Figure 25 provides a graphic overview of the recommended analytical process and outputs.

Sections VIII and IX addressed the topic of what should be done (the "analytical" dimension) in this process. This Section addresses two related topics—*who* should do it (the "management" dimension), and *when* should it be done (the "time" dimension). Figure 26 illustrates the combination of all these dimensions.

To complete the design of the system, you must define the responsibilities of individual managers in developing the profit budget, as well as specifying the timing and duration of the activities involved.

The most fundamental consideration influencing these decisions is the managerial hierarchy. In GMC, for instance, not only is there a general manager, but there are executives one level below (chief accountant, personnel manager, manufacturing manager and marketing manager) and two levels below (product managers, foremen).

Each of these executives has his own budgets and responsibility centers to manage. The firm's profit budget must recognize and integrate

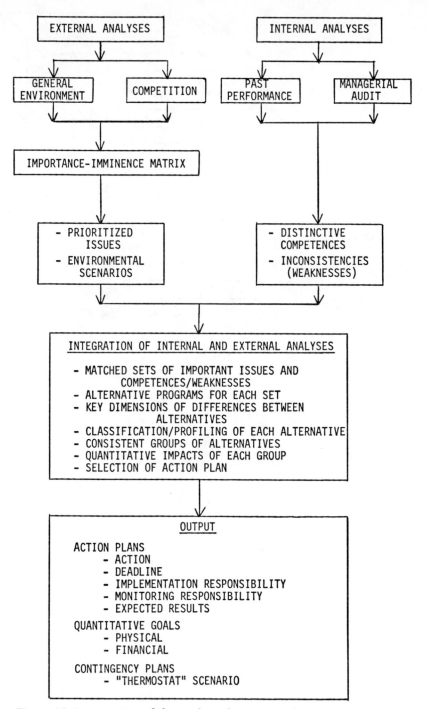

Figure 25. An overview of the analytical process and output

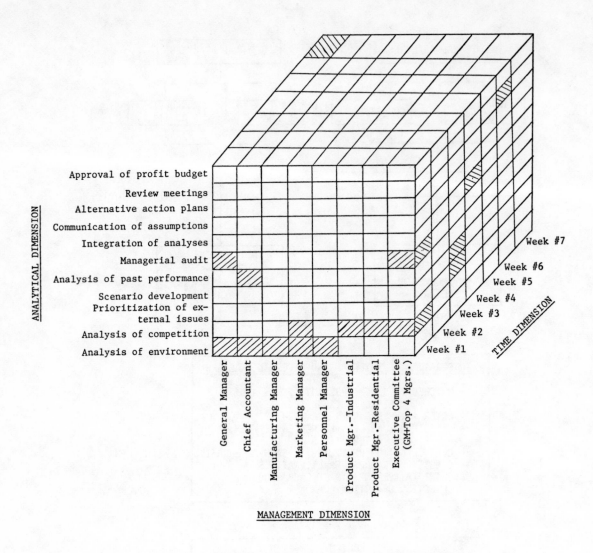

Figure 26. Model combining the analytical, management and time dimensions of the profit budgeting process

these responsibility center budgets. The basic issue is how these responsibility center budgets and the firm's budget should affect one another.

BALANCING TWO TYPES OF RELATIONSHIPS

The relationship between the firm's budget and the responsibility center budgets is complex. Should top management's goals and aspirations be the prime determinant of the content of these budgets? If the answer is yes, then a "top-down" (firm's budget → responsibility center budgets), authoritarian type of managerial involvement must be defined.

Should the departmental or functional manager's perceptions of what is feasible and what potential exists determine the firm's budget? If the answer to that question is yes, then a "bottom-up" (responsibility center budgets → firm budget), highly participative type of managerial involvement must be encouraged.

In general, neither a top-down nor bottom-up process—in its entirety—is appropriate for most firms. In most firms, *both* top management and operating management have contributions to make and insights to offer.

Top management may be more familiar with economic, regulatory, political and other environmental factors. The chief executive officer (CEO) is ordinarily more aware of and sensitive to owners'-stockholders' preferences with regard to growth and risk.

The expectations and priorities of the communities in which plants and offices are located will probably be communicated by community officials to the CEO, as will the deliberations and orientation of the company's board of directors. Most CEO's will have important contributions to make to the firm's profit plans.

Operating management would normally be most familiar with the capabilities and limitations of individual departments and the characteristics of the territories for which they are responsible. Their commitment to the achievement of the quantitative goals specified in the profit budget will be affected by their perceptions of how well the budget has incorporated the factors they consider important.

The process that should be adopted in most firms should represent a balance between the top-down and bottom-up extremes. You can accomplish such a balance by designing a series of formal communications between top management and lower level managers.

A continuing process where assumptions, plans and goals are communicated back and forth and progressively refined can exploit the insights and understanding of both top management and operating management. You can also design the process to be biased toward either the authoritarian or participative extremes. A graphic illustration of such on-going processes is shown in Figure 27.

CHOOSING THE RIGHT OPTION

Figure 27 suggests options to orient the process toward the desired authoritarian or participative extreme. In simple businesses operating in stable environments, where top management has considerable experience in the industry, and where operating management has strongly functional rather than general management expertise, a greater top-down or authoritarian bias is appropriate. In complex businesses, with highly uncertain environments, a more participative bias is usually desirable.

In some companies where the management culture is oriented toward the authoritarian mode, the process tends to be more top-down. In our opinion, the culture should reflect the type of operations and environment rather than the values of top management.

An authoritarian approach may be effectively employed for limited periods of time in firms where operating management has displayed a tendency toward complacency or lackluster performance. By specifying goals that demand a high degree of effort and competence on the part of operating management, top management can propel lower levels of management into more acceptable modes of operation.

INITIATING COMMUNICATIONS

The first communication recommended in Figure 27 is from top management to operating management. If a participative approach is desired, all that needs to be communicated is the basic assumptions of the most likely environmental scenario.

If more direction is necessary, an outline of top management's thinking about the action for the firm can be communicated in addition to the assumptions. If additional direction is to be provided, the levels

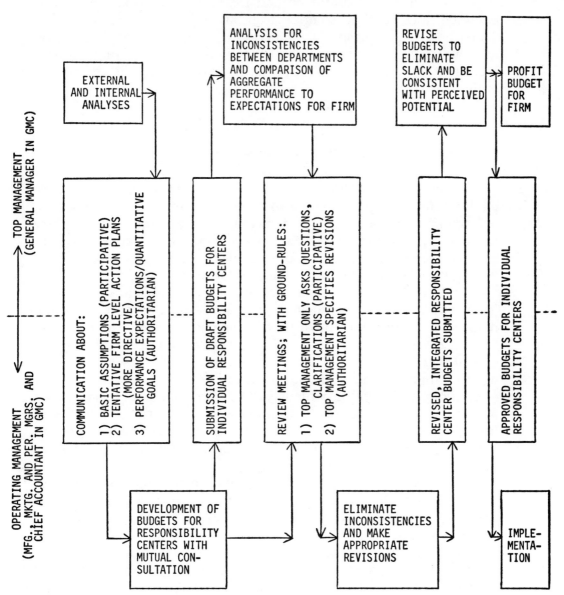

TOP-DOWN AND BOTTOM-UP PROCESSES

Figure 27. Illustration of the top-down and bottom-up management processes

of acceptable performance could be specified, in addition to the basic assumptions and the outline.

We strongly recommend that the basic assumptions *always* be communicated. This is essential to encourage consistent responsibility center budgets. If you specify the performance expectations, you should also outline the tentative action plan to indicate to operating management that these performance expectations have some basis and are not entirely arbitrary.

CONDUCTING REVIEW MEETINGS

The review meeting following the submission of the tentative responsibility center budgets should also be designed to promote the desired orientation of the process. At such meetings, many companies have very successfully employed the ground rule that top management will not exercise its authority to demand revisions in the budgets being considered, but will only ask questions and seek clarifications.

The behavioral consequences of this ground rule are very significant. First, a highly participative climate results. Second, operating management will not be embarassed by having to explicitly and publicly recognize their budgets' shortcomings. They can indicate that they will give further study or consideration to the issues raised by top management. Competent operating managers will employ the meetings as an opportunity to identify top management's preferences and orientation and implement its suggestions for improvement. Third—and this is an interesting point—top management is forced to prepare carefully before the meeting in order to identify flaws, inadequacies or inconsistencies in the budgets.

All managers reporting to top management should be present at these meetings. They are a valuable opportunity to exchange information and ideas and to promote the maximum integration and consistency of the departmental and/or functional budgets. In some firms, the review meetings are limited to an individual operating manager and to management. While this practice does reduce the pressures on the operating management, it does not enhance the communication and integration purposes of budgeting.

In the final analysis, revised budgets submitted by operating management must be modified by top management to eliminate inconsistencies and fully exploit the potential that top management believes exists: the need for such modifications should be minimal if the carefully designed recommended interactions between top management and operating management are implemented.

ASSIGNING RESPONSIBILITY FOR BUDGET PREPARATION

Five different types of functions must be carried out by a company's management to ensure the effective development of the profit budget. These five are:

1. coordinating functions;
2. analytical functions;
3. catalytic functions;
4. integrating functions; and
5. decision-making functions.

Coordinating functions largely relate to the timely management of the paper flow involved in developing the budget. You should assign one of your executives to issue the forms that have to be filled out, inform managers of the deadlines, and monitor progress toward the timely preparation of the firm's profit budget. The coordinating functions involve the management of the "time dimension" in the model pictured in Figure 26.

Part of the coordinating function might also involve providing clarifications and advice regarding the mechanics of filling in the forms. The same executive could have responsibility for the arithmetic aggregation of the information in the budget forms of responsibility centers which are destined for higher management levels.

Analytical functions involve the executions of the analyses required to prepare the budget forms. Those analyses could range from the statistical calculations required to develop standards for the lowest level responsibility centers to the study and prediction of the firm's external environment.

Most of the analytical tasks for the lower level responsibility centers can be appropriately assigned to the managers of those centers. Responsibility for other analyses such as those described in Sections VIII and IX must be carefully assigned to the most knowledgeable and competent executives you have.

MATCHING RESPONSIBILITY WITH POSITION

Certain assignments can normally be assigned to the executives whose operating responsibilities make them suitable. For example, analysis of the past financial performance of the firm can be readily assigned to the chief accountant or controller, or whoever deals with the accounting aspects of the firm's operations. At GMC, the responsibility for the financial analysis of past performance is assigned to the chief accountant.

Marketing personnel would normally be the most knowledgeable about your company's competitors. However, if the manufacturing manager or R&D personnel have significant information about competitors, they may be the appropriate persons to assign the responsibility for analyzing competition, particularly in high-technology businesses.

Components of the managerial audit can be assigned to executives belonging to different departments or functions. Topics such as organizational structure, planning and control systems, and policies would normally be assigned to senior executives who have responsibility for the firm as a whole. Alternatively, a team or committee of executives could be charged with the responsibility for conducting such an analysis.

In GMC, a committee is needed, due to the lack of senior executives with general management responsibility other than the general manager himself. The "Executive Committee" suggested in Figure 26 consists of the general manager plus the chief accountant, personnel manager, manufacturing manager and marketing manager.

The responsibility for analyzing elements of the external environment could be distributed among various executives. At GMC, political developments could be studied by the general manager himself; technological factors by the manufacturing manager; social and demographic trends by the marketing manager; economic analyses by the chief accountant; and the regulatory situation by the personnel manager. All these components of the external environment would be integrated by the Executive Committee in GMC.

In very large firms, it may be useful and effective to employ teams of executives to carry out major components of the required analyses. These teams, ideally consisting of four or five executives, would best be comprised of the seconds-in-command of the departments or functions. The executives in charge of those departments or functions tend to be less critical of the status quo than is perhaps ideal.

GOING ONE STEP FURTHER

Additional analytic tasks must be carried out when the responsibility centers submit their tentative budgets. These have to be analyzed for:

- internal consistency (e.g.: Is a 20% sales growth feasible without adding sales people?)
- mutual consistency (e.g.: Is a 20% sales growth feasible considering capacities in manufacturing?)
- consistency with the environment (e.g.: Is a 20% sales growth feasible in light of declining demand and technologically superior competitive products?)
- consistency with the firm's competences (e.g.: Is a 20% sales growth, expected on the basis of offering new products, reasonable given the R&D capabilities of the firm?)
- consistency with top management expectations (e.g.: Is a 20% sales growth in line with top management's expressed aspirations for the firm?).

These kinds of analyses are ordinarily assigned to the controller's department or accounting department in most firms. But you must ensure that the analysts possess managerial expertise rather than merely accounting knowledge.

In GMC, it might be necessary to add a budget analyst, perhaps as executive assistant to the general manager, who would possess the necessary managerial expertise and perspective. The budget analysts who check for consistency in the proposed budgets could also be usefully involved in the subsequent analyses of actual performance in relation to those budgets.

RESPONSIBILITY FOR THREE OTHER FUNCTIONS

Catalytic functions, though important, are not as tangible or as easily performed as coordinating or analytical functions. In most firms, it is necessary to encourage the creative potential of managers. This spark can be provided by an executive or executives who involve themselves deeply and extensively in the budgeting process, particularly at the analytical stage. Such an executive may not have formal responsibility or authority; he may just ask questions or make suggestions.

Effective execution of the catalytic functions requires a high degree of interpersonal skill. The executive in charge of this function should also be held in high regard by other executives in the firm. The executive assistant at GMC may be appropriate as a catalyst if he has demonstrated interpersonal competence and possesses significant managerial experience.

If you have any doubt whether an executive would discharge this responsibility with sensitivity and confidence, it would be better not to assign such a role to anyone. The catalytic function at GMC can be carried out by the general manager himself during the review meetings.

Integrating functions are less behaviorally sensitive than catalytic functions. During the process of development, the budgets of individual responsibility centers must be mutually consistent. The analyses of individual components of the environment may have implications for another component. This is where integration takes place.

In GMC, for example, the manufacturing manager's budget must be consistent with the marketing manager's sales targets, the personnel manager's recruitment plans, and the chief accountant's cash flow statement. The executive assistant could act as a communication channel to ensure the integration of these departments' budgets.

Similarly, the analysis of competition may suggest new areas of technology to explore. The importance of electronics technology to GMC's future, for instance, would not have been so readily apparent if not for the competitive developments in electronic meters. Someone in your company should consciously attempt to identify and highlight such interactions.

Decision-making functions must be clarified in many firms, particularly those introducing a formal budgeting process for the first time. Differences of opinion that require resolution or arbitration may arise in the course of developing the profit budget.

For example, the marketing manager's requirements at GMC in terms of lead times—from the provision of specifications for special-order meters to the delivery of the completed product—may appear unrealistic to the manufacturing manager, unless he has commitments from the personnel manager for recruitment of additional machinists. While the issue could be resolved by the general manager, it may be behaviorally desirable to have the concerned managers resolve their differences by negotiation rather than external arbitration.

In firms that are much larger and organizationally more complex than GMC, the responsibility for arbitrating differences that cannot be solved by negotiation may have to be specified for issues that arise frequently.

THE FINAL RESPONSIBILITY

There is one decision-making responsibility that, in our opinion, is extremely clear. The responsibility for the final revisions and approval of the budget for a company cannot and should not be delegated or diluted by the CEO. He is responsible to the owners or shareholders for the firm's performance. It would be inappropriate for this crucial authority to be delegated to executives who do not morally and explicitly shoulder this responsibility.

THE TIME DIMENSION

There are three important time-related decisions you must make when designing the profit budgeting system. The first—already discussed—is the time horizon that the budget should cover. The two other decisions are the duration of the process of developing the budget and the frequency with which the budget development exercise should be repeated.

When determining the appropriate duration of the budget development process, three considerations are important. The first two suggest a duration as short as possible. For one, when the budget development process takes a long time, momentum and executive commitment are often lost. The resulting perception is that too much time is being taken up by the process to the detriment of other managerial responsibilities.

For another, the longer the duration of the process, the greater the probability that the basic assumptions and scenarios will prove inappropriate or obsolete. A firm that devotes six months to the process probably develops its basic assumptions in July, assuming that the fiscal and calendar years coincide. The final budget may be completed in early December. If the firm had devoted only two months to the process, it would develop its assumptions in October, with a great deal more reliability and accuracy.

Balanced against these arguments is the need to provide a reasonable amount of time for the necessary analysis. You'll have to make judgments about the appropriate minimum time. But your bias should be strongly toward as short a duration as possible. *If no complaints are heard from operating managers about inadequate time to develop the budget, the duration is almost certainly too long.*

DETERMINING THE FREQUENCY OF BUDGET DEVELOPMENT REPETITION

The final important time-related design decision is the frequency of the exercise. It is evident that the recommended process is quite demanding in terms of managerial time and effort.

If your firm already possesses a strategic planning system, much of the analysis recommended in Sections VIII and IX would be carried out as part of that planning exercise.

In the absence of such a system, the recommended process provides the firm with the required strategic orientation for developing the budget. But to carry out the recommended process annually—in its totality—as part of the strategic planning system or the profit budgeting system has proven to be unnecessary and perhaps even undesirable.

The recommended process *must* be carried out fully the first year in which the profit budgeting system is put in place in the firm. You will find it largely redundant to repeat the entire exercise the following year, however.

In GMC, for instance, the general manager and his proposed executive assistant (with some assistance, if necessary) should review the basic assumptions and scenarios. These will usually require some minor modifications. Strengths and weaknesses of the company are monitored and updated through the review and follow-up process described in Section XI. It should be a simple matter, therefore, to issue an updated communication to start the budgeting process in the second year.

A full-fledged analytical exercise involving all the other executives is unlikely to provide enough additional benefits or insights to justify the cost of the executives' time and effort.

In the third year, it may again be adequate for the general manager and his aide to assume the responsibility for updating the basic assumptions and external scenarios. A year later—in the fourth year—it may be worthwhile to repeat the comprehensive exercise.

On occasion you may find it desirable to initiate a full-fledged exercise a year or two ahead of schedule if major, sudden or unexpected changes take place that warrant a complete re-statement of basic assumptions, environmental scenarios and the firm's action plan.

Figure 28 clarifies the suggested frequency for the budgeting exercise.

ACTION REQUIREMENTS

The action requirements described here relate to the last three Sections. The recommended action sequence is quite different from the sequence employed to describe the budget *development* process.

The first step is to determine the operating cycle of the business. The impact period of key operating decisions, such as advertising, should be studied. This step is described at the beginning of Section IX.

Based on the determination of the operating cycle and the impact period of operating decisions, the second step is to determine the time horizon of the profit budget. Table 8 in Section IX suggests the appropriate time horizon based on the operating cycle.

The third step is to design the forms to document the output of the analytical process. These would include:

- the format for the firm's action plan
- the format for the quantitative goals of the firm, derived from the CEO's performance report and including necessary financial statements

RECOMMENDED FREQUENCY OF THE BUDGETING EXERCISE
GENERAL METERS CORPORATION

YEAR OF PREPARATION/DURATION	HORIZON YEAR	RECOMMENDED PROCESS
1983 Two months' duration	1985	Comprehensive analysis with extensive participation resulting in complete revision of assumptions, scenarios, and firm's action plan.
1984 One month's duration	1986	Review and selective updating of assumptions and environmental scenario by small top-management team.
1985 One month's duration	1987	Review and selective updating of assumptions and environmental scenario by small top-management team.
1986 Two months' duration	1988	Comprehensive analysis with extensive participation resulting in complete revision of assumptions, scenarios and firm's action plan.

Figure 28. Recommended time frequency for GMC's budgeting exercise

- and the format for the contingency plans, which would be similar to, but in less detail than, the formats for the action plan and quantitative goals.

You can determine which kind of contingency plan is suitable to your firm at this time, as discussed in Section IX.

The fourth step is to define the analytical process that you want to carry out. Figure 22 in Section VIII and Figure 25 in Section X provide an overview of the total process.

The fifth step is to determine the appropriate bias toward a bottom-up or top-down process based on the characteristics of your firm (described in Section X). Figure 27 in Section X indicates the options available that enable you to design the process with the appropriate bias.

The sixth step is to detail the analyses you want carried out (as described in Section VIII) and to assign the responsibility for these analyses to individual executives or to teams of executives.

At this time, you should assign the responsibility for coordinating and integrating functions, and assess the possibility of an executive or executives accomplishing the catalytic functions. These coordinating, analytical, catalytic, and integrating functions are discussed in Section X.

You may develop a preliminary definition of the decision-making function at this time. But a satisfactory definition is usually possible only when the process is being executed for the first time.

The seventh step is to determine the appropriate duration of the process, as discussed in Section X. It should then be possible to develop a model of the system, like the one diagrammed in Figure 26 of that Section.

Finally, you must tentatively decide on the frequency with which the comprehensive exercise is to be carried out. A firmer determination can be made after the system has been in operation for two years. You should also identify the top-management team assigned the responsibility for the updating of assumptions and scenarios in the years between full-fledged exercises.

The recommended profit budgeting system is not complete without the design and implementation of the crucially important review and follow-up process discussed in the next Section. And the final building block for a successful program will be the behavioral and managerial considerations pertinent to the effective design and implementation of the recommended system as discussed in Section XII.

XI

Guidelines for Performance Review

It has traditionally been felt that the top-down or bottom-up orientation of the process of formulating the budget is the single most important behavioral consideration when designing the budgeting system.

We recently conducted research projects which looked at the systems in about 90 companies. That analysis indicated that an equally important behavioral consideration is the review and follow-up exercise.

DESIGNING THE FOLLOW-UP SYSTEM

The comparison and analysis of actual performance in relation to the budget, and the initiation and monitoring of remedial action are important determinants of the perceived effectiveness of the management control system. On the basis of in-depth interviews with executives in companies with effective systems, we identified the key guidelines to ensure an effective review and follow-up process.

The importance of a well-designed and executed performance review was continually reinforced. Systems that have been extremely well-designed in other respects often fail because of poorly executed performance reviews. At the same time, systems of mediocre design in some respects perform quite satisfactorily if the performance review is well executed.

The quality of the performance analysis and the manner in which you carry it out can provide strong signals about your management's commitment to using the budgeting system effectively. The recommended guidelines incorporate vital behavioral implications of the way in which the review is carried out.

In particular, you should keep in mind the resulting attitudes of lower-level managers and their approach to subsequent budget formulation processes. The profit budget is both a planning and a control tool. Top management's approach to exercising control can greatly influence the creativity and attitudes to openness and risk-taking on the part of lower level managers in later planning exercises.

DECIDING ON FREQUENCY OF REVIEW

To a large degree, the nature of operations in the responsibility center determines the frequency with which performance should be reviewed by the manager of that center and his superior. You should review the characteristics of the responsibility center which determine the frequency of formal performance reports. Those same characteristics largely determine the frequency with which formal joint reviews should be scheduled.

While daily and weekly reports may be generated at lower levels in the organization, most of the important responsibility centers generate reports on a monthly basis. Consequently, joint reviews cannot ordinarily be scheduled more often than that.

In situations where the environment is stable, departmental-functional managers are competent, the product line has been in existence for years, and no significant changes in these considerations are expected, you might only schedule meetings between the CEO and department heads once every quarter.

INCORPORATING ADAPTIVE CONTROL

Some modern executives encourage what is called "adaptive control." The budgets that you develop aim to identify profit potential available.

But as time passes, a better understanding of what that potential actually is might emerge.

In such situations, you may encourage managers to adapt or modify their originally planned actions and decisions to best exploit that improved understanding. When you implement adaptive control, you can assess performance not only in relation to the budgets, but also in relation to the best performance that could have been accomplished, given the improved understanding that was developed.

Adaptive control is a difficult process to implement successfully in the majority of budget situations. It demands a high degree of trust and mutual respect between superiors and subordinates at all levels in the organization. It also requires highly effective communications between departmental-functional managers so that the needed integration of their respective actions can be maintained. These managers must be committed to the company's goals rather than to the performance goals of their individual departments.

Adaptive control is not suited to every organization. In firms where the necessary conditions exist, adaptive control has functioned effectively and helped reduce the frequency of formal reviews.

DELINEATING THE ROLE OF THE SUPERIOR

The attitude of the executive participating in each formal joint performance review greatly influences the exercise. In fact, our experience indicates that the climate that exists during these reviews has a substantial impact on the managerial climate of the company as a whole.

The superior can make the review process an uncomfortable exercise apportioning blame for shortcomings in performance. Or he can make the review process a productive collaborative effort where both superior and subordinate apply their insights and abilities to the task of improving future performance.

Both the superior and subordinate have distinctive and valuable contributions to make. The superior possesses a broader organizational perspective of the reasons for, and implications of, the performance of the subordinate's responsibility center. The subordinate is close to where the action is. He can provide a detailed and first-hand understanding that may not be reflected in the performance reports.

When deciding on remedial action, the superior must determine when the subordinate's suggestions and preferences should be accepted and when they should be modified. Barring exceptional circumstances, a superior should accept most of a subordinate's preferences with regard to remedial action.

FOCUSING ON EXCEPTIONAL CIRCUMSTANCES

There are at least three exceptional circumstances, however, where the superior has the obligation to overrule the subordinate.

First, if the subordinate's plans are clearly inappropriate, based on erroneous assumptions, or do not take into account information available to the superior, the executive should exercise his authority if the subordinate does not appear to be open to reason or persuasion.

Second, it a continuing trend over two or three formal reviews indicates that the subordinate's remedial actions and plans are consistently ineffective, the superior should assume a more direct and substantial responsibility for identifying and implementing remedial action. The importance of keeping track of trends is obvious.

Third, if there are remedial actions that fall within the superior's capability but that lie outside the formal authority of the subordinate, it would be reasonable and appropriate that the superior become directly involved at an early stage. An example of such actions would be the transferring of resources, such as personnel, from other responsibility centers to the responsibility center that is experiencing difficulty.

Except for those circumstances discussed above, it is generally best to allow the subordinate to select and implement remedial actions.

RESPONDING TO DEVIATIONS

Many major companies follow a pattern of responses to deviations that parallels those recommendations. There is a graduated assumption of responsibility by the superior executive. Poor performance by the subordinate over one or two review periods is left largely to the subordinate to resolve. The possibility exists that this poor performance may be the result of random occurrences and will disappear.

Also, the subordinate must be given the opportunity to correct the situation. You presume that most have the competence to do so. It would be overly demanding on the superior and would not be utilizing the subordinate's capabilities if all deviations were treated as the superior's direct responsibility.

If the deviation continues for three or more review periods, the superior gives explicit directions to the subordinate on the appropriate remedial actions to take. At this time, the superior identifies remedial actions which are within his power to implement, but are beyond the bounds of the subordinate's formal authority.

Finally, if the problem continues, it becomes the superior's immediate and direct responsibility to correct the situation. If the problem is significant enough, progressively higher levels of the organization get involved.

You should make sure that your review process emphasizes the management control problem of identifying reasons for deviation of performance from the budget and instituting required remedial action. The main focus should not be the personnel problem of evaluating the subordinate's shortcomings and appropriate future development.

The ideal situation would be to separate the review process from the personnel evaluation and development issue. It is not feasible, however, to ignore entirely personnel evaluation considerations when conducting the review and follow-up exercise.

But you should make every effort to minimize personnel evaluation considerations during the review and follow-up process.

DETERMINING THE ROLE OF THE SUBORDINATE

The superior's approach largely dictates the subordinate's role and behavior. If the superior adopts a fault-finding stance, the subordinate is likely to be wary, defensive and not entirely candid. If the superior emphasizes collaborative problem-solving, the subordinate will be encouraged to be open, frank and creative in identifying remedial actions.

The subordinate must decide whether deviations from budgets are caused by erroneous assumptions, improper goals, ineffective action plans or poor implementation. This determination of the probable primary cause of deviations has a major impact on the appropriate managerial response.

If erroneous assumptions are the problem, you may need to review the entire budget, including the goals and action plans. If the goals are improper or unfeasible, then both goals and action plans may have to be revised. If the action plans are ineffective, you must seek alternative means of accomplishing the stated goals. If poor implementation is the key, the manager must review his own behavior and efforts as the key to improving the situation.

In order for the adaptive control approach to be successful, subordinates must view it as a recognition of their competence and as a challenge to achieve better than budgeted performance if the opportunity arises. The uncertainty under which they operate in an adaptive situation is greater than in a solely budget-oriented control situation.

If the subordinates do not perceive that the adaptive control practices at review time reflect their superior's confidence in their capabilities, the adaptive control process will not work.

COPING WITH UNCERTAINTY

The recommended profit budgeting system is designed to recognize and reduce the uncertainties that can cause actual performance to deviate from budgeted performance. Those uncertainties can affect managerial performance. Even the most competent and committed managers will inevitably encounter situations where—despite their best efforts—the performance of their responsibility centers fall short of budgeted expectations. You must recognize this possibility in your review exercise.

There are several modes of action the superior executive can take. First, he can tell the subordinate that the budgeted expectations have to be met regardless of the problems encountered. Second, he can accept and operate on revised expectations for the remaining period until the budget is formally updated. But he can still base rewards and penalties on the original budget expectations. Third, he can agree to revise budget expectations and base rewards and penalties on the revised figures. Each of these responses is appropriate in specific situations.

TAILORING EXECUTIVE RESPONSES TO SPECIFIC SITUATIONS

If the assumptions on which the budget was developed continue to be perceived as valid—and if there is the possibility that the subordinate can solve the problem in the remaining time before a formally updated budget goes into operation—then the superior should not revise the budget. In other words, if the cause of the deviations is not erroneous assumptions or improper or unfeasible goals, you should not revise the budget.

If the shortcomings are due to poor implementation of the action plan, then the year-end goals should definitely not be revised. You can assign the subordinate who is responsible for the poor performance higher targets for the remaining period so the originally set goals for the budget period are achieved.

If the assumptions on which the budget was based prove to be wrong, it may be appropriate to revise the goals and action plans. You may want to retain the financial goals by modifying the action plan to respond to the changed set of assumptions. Under such circumstances, where you've found the assumptions erroneous, it may even be best to link incentives to the revised targets.

In the final analysis, the superior must make an assessment of the impact of revised budgets on subordinates' behavior. If revising the budget will appear fair and reasonable and motivate subordinates to greater efforts, then the budget should be revised. However, if not revising the budgets is likely to encourage the subordinates to greater efforts, then it may be desirable to retain the original budgets even if they are perceived as unreasonable.

EXECUTIVE GUIDELINES FOR BUDGET REVIEW

There are a few demonstrably effective guidelines that every superior should keep in mind to ensure an effective review and follow-up exercise.

First, evaluate subordinates with reference to the potential available. If the adaptive control approach is likely to work in the firm, adopt it. If not, performance should be evaluated only with reference to the budget.

The common practice of comparing one manager's performance

to another's is highly undesirable. Such a comparison is desirable at the planning stage, when the budget is being developed, so that improved practices can be adopted. Comparison when performance is being evaluated is unproductive.

Second, always take into consideration the quality and magnitude of the efforts made by the subordinate. No budgeting system can identify potential with absolute certainty. When actual performance falls short of the budget, it may happen despite the best efforts of competent managers. Subordinates appreciate the reassurance that their superiors recognize that they have done an excellent job despite unfavorable variances on their performances reports.

Third, emphasize tracking trends. You can better analyze the reasons for deviations by analyzing trends than by considering performance for just one reporting period. Also, the response by the superior should take into account the duration over which the problem has been experienced. A random single period problem may be best ignored. A continuing multi-period problem calls for progressively greater involvement of the superior in correcting the situation.

Fourth, stress the collaborative character of the review process, the fact that it is a joint effort on the part of superior and subordinate to analyze and remedy unsatisfactory performance. If the review process becomes an exercise in apportioning blame, the basic purpose of correcting the situation is not effectively served.

Fifth, record and monitor remedial actions decided on in an initial review process when it is time for subsequent reviews. Use the format for action plans to document and monitor the effectiveness of the planned remedial actions.

UTILIZING FORMS FROM THE BUDGET PROCESS IN FOLLOW-UP ACTIVITIES

Certain features of the recommended profit budgeting system have been designed to support and improve the review and follow-up process.

The action plans that are the basis of the budget are very valuable to determine the probable cause of shortfalls in performance. If the planned actions were not promptly or correctly implemented, it is probable that inadequate managerial effort is the reason for poor performance.

If the actions were all implemented in a timely fashion, but the results are still poor, you should closely scrutinize the validity of the goals and the appropriateness of the original action plans. Comprehensive financial and non-financial goals—in addition to a detailed action plan—are also very important in the context of the review and follow-up process.

The recommended contingency plans are also important. The scenario approach, in particular, is a powerful technique to monitor the appropriateness of key assumptions and to reduce the lead time for identifying needed changes in the action plan to respond to the changed assumptions.

Finally, the explicit identification of key assumptions by top management during the process of formulating the budget is vital to the review process. Without consistency and agreement between superior and subordinate concerning the assumptions on which the budget is based, attempts to develop a common understanding of the reasons for deviations are likely to be unsuccessful.

ACTION REQUIREMENTS

The first decision you must make is the frequency of meetings required of the manager of each responsibility center with his superior. At GMC, these meetings could be scheduled at monthly intervals in the week immediately following the report for the previous period. The meetings at each successively higher level should be scheduled in sequence so that each manager has an opportunity to discuss performance with his subordinates before meeting his superior.

It may be necessary to specify additional participants at some review meetings. The general manager at GMC, for instance, could benefit from the analytical services of the executive assistant.

Guidelines should be formally stated and required. The five key guidelines include evaluating against potential, evaluating effort, tracking trends, collaborative efforts and formal monitoring of the remedial action.

The possibility of adopting the practice of adaptive control should be examined after a year or two of experience with the budgeting system. The behavioral constraints on the applicability of adaptive control are likely to be more difficult to overcome than the technical problems. Therefore, the attitudes of lower-level managers should be the primary consideration when examining the feasibility of adaptive control.

XII

Implementing Your Own Budgeting System

The "action requirements" at the end of each chapter summarize the largely technical design decisions that you must make. This Section discusses other practical considerations that can contribute to the effectiveness of your system.

The three basic additional areas are:

- the question that is asked repeatedly—"Who should design the system?"
- the issue of how to introduce the new system, quickly or over a long period
- the matter of assessing how well the system is functioning.

WHO SHOULD DESIGN THE SYSTEM?

The most important issue in designing the system is the role of the CEO. The CEO must visibly demonstrate his commitment to the system if it is to succeed. This commitment must be expressed in the following ways:

1. Initiate or fully support the design and introduction of the new system.

2. Understand the benefits and limitations of the new system, so that reasonable expectations about its contributions to the firm's performance are developed.

3. Ensure the availability of needed design resources. Assign appropriate executives to the task of designing and introducing the system. Obtain outside technical assistance if needed. And participate in key design decisions, such as the top-down or bottom-up bias to incorporate in the process of formulating the budget.

4. Provide the resources needed to administer the system when it is in place. Appoint executives to carry out the various functions discussed in Section X.

5. Use the system as the firm's primary vehicle for planning and control and actively participate in review meetings to analyze performance reports.

APPOINTING A DESIGN TEAM

The most effective approach we have found for designing the system is for the CEO to appoint a team of executives to carry out the task. This team should, if at all possible, include the executive in the firm most responsible for promoting the idea of the new system, if the idea was not originally conceived by the CEO. The team should not exceed five or, at most, six executives.

The team members should possess a varied range of expertise. The accounting and MIS functions should be represented, as well as line managers from key departments. The team members should have an in-depth understanding of the existing company's management systems and existing operations, and should be able to communicate that knowledge.

They bear the responsibility to educate and convince other managers in the firm about the characteristics and benefits of the system. They should therefore be highly regarded executives who are viewed by their colleagues and superiors as competent and trustworthy.

If it is not possible to spare the time of the firm's executives to design the system, then an outside consultant may be necessary. Outside consultants who do not work closely with an in-house team in designing and installing the system are often not effective, however. Regardless of the consultant's technical expertise and experience, each firm's history and characteristics are different. Experienced company executives have insights, understanding and knowledge about sources of information that the consultant needs. Also, the consultant's services are not available indefinitely, and an in-house understanding of the rationale for design choices that have been made is required.

This understanding becomes necessary when modifications to the system emerge due to inevitable changes in the characteristics of the firm and its environment. By working closely with a consultant, an in-house team can provide valuable help *and* develop useful knowledge about the system. Also, when introducing the system, the members of the in-house team provide a core of committed and knowledgeable executives to convince their colleagues about the benefits of the new system.

This book was written so that an in-house team, without significant technical expertise, can design and install the system without the assistance of consultants. We strongly recommend that the design of the system be substantially, if not totally, an in-house effort.

INTRODUCING THE SYSTEM

The basic questions for introducing the system are a) whether a phased approach is necessary and b) if needed, how that phasing should take place. Phasing is necessary if:

1. the firm is extremely large (over \$100 million in annual sales, several hundred or more employees) and complex (several different product lines, multiple manufacturing locations, many sales territories); and
2. formal planning and control systems in existence are rudimentary or non-existent.

You can phase in the introduction of your system in one of two ways. The system can be gradually implemented over a long-term period, sometimes as long as two or three years. Or you can introduce the system in selected segments of the firm, implementing it in subsequent years in remaining segments of the firm.

If you adopt phasing because of the size and complexity of the firm, then a segment approach is best. The segment approach, however, does not permit the comprehensive profit-planning exercise detailed in Sections VIII, IX and X. In each segment, the appropriate departmental-functional responsibility center budgets described in Section V, VI, VII have to be implemented first. After you implement these responsibility center budgets in the remaining segments, the comprehensive, firm-wide profit-planning process can be introduced.

CHOOSING SEGMENTS FOR PHASING

In selecting the segment of the firm where the initial implementation is to take place, top management must make a conscious choice between segments that are relatively simple to handle and those that are likely to give rise to problems.

If top management senses a need to demonstrate the viability and benefits of the new system, the difficult segments should be tackled first. That creates a positive and significant impact on the attitudes of the executives in the firm.

If the organizational climate is favorable to the introduction of more effective management systems, then the easier segments can be addressed first. This enables the design team to gradually build the confidence and practical understanding necessary to efficiently address the more difficult segments.

ORDER OF INSTALLATION OF ACTIVITIES

If the lack of prior experience with formal management systems is the reason for phasing, a careful step-by-step introduction of the profit budgeting system is necessary. You should design and install the reporting system first. The development of standards and performance expectations can be postponed for a few months until managers are familiar with the content of the reports. Performance in the same month or period of the previous year, if available, can be reported as a substitute for more meaningful benchmarks.

One you build up a historical record, you can then start setting standards. Budgets for individual responsibility centers can be developed, essentially using past performance as a guide. Then you can introduce the comprehensive profit budgeting process for the firm a year later after managers have developed a formal understanding of the impact of resource levels on performance, relationships with other responsibility centers, and the decisions that have been made. Workshops or discussion sessions in which the design team explains the purposes and operation of the system to other executives are very valuable in facilitating implementation.

ASSESSING THE SYSTEM'S EFFECTIVENESS

After the new profit-budgeting system has been in operation for a year or more, it is desirable to evaluate the system to make improvements in subsequent budgeting cycles. A senior executive or team of executives can adequately accomplish this task. If a team is assigned, it should be a small group of three or four. One or two, but not all, of its members should have been on the team that was responsible for designing and implementing the system.

You may find an outside consultant particularly valuable when conducting the evaluation exercise. Executives who may not be entirely open when interviewed by a colleague often tend to communicate with outsiders with less hesitation.

An objective observer has less involvement in the politics of managing the firm. Executives may perceive the outsider as an individual who can better understand and appreciate their points of view. Also, the consultant can easily and effectively offer the assurance of confidentiality. Such an assurance is not as meaningful when offered by an executive from within the firm.

THE SCOPE OF THE EVALUATION

Throughout the evaluation of the profit budgeting system, you must ensure that the emphasis lies in improving the system, not criticizing the efforts of the executives who designed and implemented it.

The sources of information should include the formal documentation of the process of formulation and the output of the budget, as well as interviews with executives involved with the system. Any executive who wishes to offer his reactions to the system should be given the opportunity to do so by the review team. In large organizations, a questionnaire-based survey of executives' reactions to the system is often useful.

You must proceed with caution, however, when carrying out the evaluation. The system itself creates pressures for improved performance. Often executives react to these pressures or to the analytical and management skills and competence demanded of them by the system, rather than to the question of how to improve the system.

The evaluation should be wide-ranging in its scope and include at least the following four areas.

First, assess the appropriateness of the analytical, management and time dimensions of the process that was employed to formulate the budget. Compare the actual process to what the designers had intended and then to what is recommended in this book. Ask:

- Were the analyses comprehensive?
- Were the right personnel involved?
- Was the time allowed appropriate?

Second, examine the outputs of the process. Ask:

- Was the profit budget comprehensive?
- Did it include all recommended elements of the action plans, quantitative goals and contingency plans?
- Was the matching of environmental issues with the firm's capabilities and limitations thorough?
- Did the action plans represent the conscious selection of the best alternatives from sets of meaningful and creative options?
- Were the standards employed in responsibility center budgets appropriately and effectively developed?
- Were the parameters and measures of performance suitable and did they include the critical variables?
- Were remedial measures documented and monitored as part of the review and follow-up process?
- Were the goals that were set too high or too easily attained?
- Were the assumptions that were made valid?

- Were needed modifications to the assumptions and related marginal changes in the profit budget identified in the years between the comprehensive exercise?

Third, evaluate the spin-off or fringe benefits of the system. Ask:

- Do managers now better understand the various forces that influence their performances?
- Are the interrelationships and communications between responsibility centers understood and handled better than they were prior to the system?
- Do managers feel that the system has provided them with a learning experience, broader perspectives about the organization, and improved insights regarding their own operations?
- Do managers feel that they have better relationships with their colleagues, subordinates, and superiors?

A FINAL KEY AREA

The fourth area you must examine could have been covered under the outputs of the system discussed earlier. However, it is key to evaluating the effectiveness of the budgeting system. Also, it is different from the previous emphases of evaluation in that it does not directly lead to improvements in the system design, only to understanding whether the present design is useful. Consequently, we consider it separately from the evaluation of the outputs of the system.

In this aspect of the evaluation, the reviewing executive or team should attempt to identify areas of potential and plans of action that would not have been identified and developed if the profit budgeting system had not been implemented. Ask:

- Have successful new product ideas emerged?
- Has customer service and satisfaction improved?
- Has market share increased?
- Have new applications for existing products and new customers or customer types been identified?

In the final analysis, if the profit budgeting system does not improve your firm's profits and prospects for profits in the future, it has not served its primary purpose. The profit budgeting system described in this book is designed with the fundamental objective of enabling your firm to identify and exploit its profit potential more effectively than it has in the past. Our experiences with the recommended system strongly suggest that it will accomplish this objective.

Index

Page numbers in **bold** type indicate information in tables and figures.